"This is the book I wish I had when I decided to reinvent myself and start my own side hustle. I spent my entire professional career in higher education. I never thought about some of the important questions raised in Carrie and Craig's book around subjects such as "finding your Who" and "designing a Life Vision." Just understanding the magnitude of these two topics alone, and how to approach them, can fundamentally change a person's life.

The breadth and depth covered in this book will help you understand what's necessary when starting and profiting from a side hustle, including those who already have a business but want to take it the next level. Reading the book feels like having two mentors working with you, side by side, with specific steps and guidelines to ensure your success.

In a nutshell, I cannot recommend this book enough. Get a copy now."

—**DR. AI ADDYSON-ZHANG,** professor turned entrepreneur, CEO of ClassroomWithoutWalls.ai, and author of *Skip the Tuition, Save the Money*

"Carrie and Craig have created a framework for taking action in the direction of your dreams. They've presented a structured approach to launch a sustainable side hustle that can take your life to the next level. Their voices both weave in and out of the story as your guides and mentors along the way. This one is a game changer and deserves a place on every aspiring entrepreneur's bookshelf."

—**CHRIS DECKER,** cofounder and CCO of Salescast, Inc. and author of *PROF!T*

SO YOU WANT TO START A SIDE HUSTLE

**BUILD A BUSINESS THAT
EMPOWERS YOU TO
LIVE YOUR LIFE, *YOUR WAY***

CARRIE BOHLIG AND CRAIG CLICKNER

New York Chicago San Francisco Athens London Madrid
Mexico City Milan New Delhi Singapore Sydney Toronto

1 2 3 4 5 6 7 8 9   LCR   26 25 24 23 22 21

ISBN   978-1-264-25868-0
MHID   1-264-25868-2

e-ISBN   978-1-264-25869-7
e-MHID   1-264-25869-0

Library of Congress Cataloging-in-Publication Data

Names: Clickner, Craig, author. | Bohlig, Carrie, author.
Title: So you want to start a side hustle : build a business that empowers
    you to live your life, your way / Craig Clickner and Carrie Bohlig.
Description: 1 Edition. | New York City : McGraw Hill, 2021. |
    Includes bibliographical references and index.
Identifiers: LCCN 2020054845 (print) | LCCN 2020054846 (ebook) |
    ISBN 9781264258680 (hardback) | ISBN 9781264258697 (ebook)
Subjects: LCSH: New business enterprises. | New business
    enterprises—Planning.
Classification: LCC HD62.5 .C595 2021 (print) | LCC HD62.5 (ebook) |
    DDC 658.1/1—dc23
LC record available at https://lccn.loc.gov/2020054845
LC ebook record available at https://lccn.loc.gov/2020054846

McGraw Hill books are available at special quantity discounts to use as premiums and sales promotions or for use in corporate training programs. To contact a representative, please visit the Contact Us pages at www.mhprofessional.com.

To our amazing parents and sisters, thank you for being remarkable living examples of what the world needs more of. We have been *so blessed* by your **love**.

To our mentors and business partners, thank you for your constant support, **patience**, and willingness to push the boundaries on what is possible. To go through life with people of your caliber is *our* honor.

And to our children, Elouise and Augusten, may you have the **courage**, kindness, and most important, the character to make an *honest* run at it. Life, that is.

CONTENTS

INTRODUCTION

From Craig

One of the greatest adventures and most rewarding accomplishments of starting our side hustles was manifesting the ability to step away from corporate America. Not only did we generate the income we needed, but we created the time we craved. Of all the goals worth pursuing, fighting for the life you want to live should be one of the highest priorities.

Our time is finite and has no return policy. It cannot be replaced, redeemed, or even exchanged for store credit. But money, on the other hand, can be made and lost . . . and even remade. Why so many of us spend our lives trading a more valuable precious asset for a less valuable asset is an important question. While I have always appreciated and even enjoyed working hard and earning money, I do not enjoy *trading my life for it*. My guess, if you picked up this book, you may feel similarly.

My journey to address this issue started back in college by studying finance and economics—with the specific intention of saving up enough money in my late twenties that I could step away from the corporate world, claim a humble financial independence, and "walk the earth" like Samuel L. Jackson's character in *Pulp Fiction*.

However, as I became a young professional, what seemed like the solution was to simply focus on *increasing my rate of pay*. Unfortunately, this doesn't solve the time-money paradox. In fact, in our culture, the more we earn, the more susceptible we are to the dangers of overspending and the never-ending spiral of making more money to buy more stuff, rinse and repeat, always wondering why happiness or security is elusive and just one more pay raise away.

I have come to understand that, despite the clever saying to the contrary, *time is not money*. Time and money are, however, interrelated and have always been so.

So with my degrees and a good job at Deutsche Bank in hand, I ventured off to the corporate world to work hard, live humbly, and save, save, save. I lived with my parents for several months and eventually moved in with some friends—agreeing to live in a condominium mechanical closet barely large enough to hold the furnace and a double mattress. Safe? Unlikely. Economical? Yes.

With a modest amount of savings and a small loan (with interest) from my parents, I bought a condo at 24 years old, rented out three rooms on the top floor, and lived in the basement. My monthly cash flow was *zero*—but I had a free place to live and was building equity. Side note: I bought that condo for $132,000 and 14 years later sold it for $115,000. Buy high, sell *low*? Clearly, I was no real estate prodigy.

Simultaneously I began pursuing an MBA, and strategically, my employer (GE) was footing the bill. However, I came to realize I only wanted a master's degree because I'd been incubating in academia for 17-plus years, conditioned to think more education was the path to getting ahead.

So despite a handful of promotions, pursuing an MBA, being a homeowner, and investing what little was left in the stock market, like many recent grads, I became disheartened. Willing to do everything right in my pursuit of a remarkable life, *I was still in an unwinnable boxing match against math itself.* My goal was to amass $500,000 of investable assets, earn a conservative 5 percent interest, and generate a financial independence "salary" of $25,000/year. However, with a salary of $34,000 a year, living economically, and saving $8,000 a year, how long would it take to get to $500,000? The answer: not acceptable.

Financial independence was not going to happen at a young age unless I started buying stocks on margin (borrowed money) or won the lottery. I didn't have the guts to go all in on the stock market, and playing the lottery always felt like an extra tax on people who are bad at math. Working "harder" in my job was not the answer. So in the end I had one choice: *Side hustle it up,* or toss my dream of stepping away from a traditional job at an untraditional age out with the trash.

Although frustrated, I was also determined, and open minded. I just didn't know WHAT to do. That's when, by fortune, fate, or divine intervention, I stumbled upon the right WHO. I met some business owners in their late twenties and early thirties who had built side hustles to the tune of several million in revenue—and had stepped away from their corporate jobs. I was both dubious and captivated.

In contrast to my corporate bosses, my family, and friends, these entrepreneurs not only knew how to create the financial success I was looking for, they also had the overall lifestyle I envisioned for myself. By gaining their mentorship, the trajectory of my life shifted. Instead of focusing on WHAT I needed to do with little guidance or mindset, I could dial in on the WHO, which over time taught me the HOW. Most important, I had *real live examples*—the dream was real. Through this association, and in a frenzied haze of working long hours in my job and moonlighting with my initial side hustles in the evening, I met and fell deeply in love with Carrie Bohlig. (This is where our side hustle story turns love story—but we will spare you that love story for now.)

From Carrie

As a women's studies and sociology college student, and shortly after, a full-time teacher turned entrepreneur, I always daydreamed about writing a book on the lessons learned and changes made during the wild entrepreneurial odyssey called my twenties.

My thought process began to shift as I was transitioning from collegiate life to adulting. My dad wined and dined me (meaning he fed me pizza) and emphasized the importance of having more than one way to make money. It was casual but cautionary, and his advice connected the dots for me that if I genuinely wanted to create an exceptional life, I had to go out of bounds on the mainstream "go to school and get a good job" adage.

Since I was not hardcore enough to quit my job and attempt to gut out a startup, nor did I have genuine business expertise, I instead jumped into the world of *moderate entrepreneurship*, meaning I launched my first side hustle.

Fast-forward into my thirties, and that approach allowed me to walk out of my career decades sooner than had I taken the conventional path, being able to travel the world, experiencing life as an adventure, and creating a home life with our children that I wouldn't trade for anything. And most important, it's given me the opportunity to invest into others in a way I had always hoped for, as my goal was *never* just to make a bunch of money, but to create significance.

Through this journey, it dawned on us that there's *not* enough guidance out there for side hustlers who have to keep their career afloat, manage their life, all while navigating building a business. Thus this book.

I always pictured authors taking months abroad to ponder and write, amid beautiful country landscapes, quill and ink in one hand and a glass of red in the other. As you may have guessed, that is *not* how writing this book played out for *me*. I more often than not had a toddler pulling on my leg as I maintained a tight-enough grip on my laptop to reassure myself that the "All changes saved in Drive" button was lit up [insert deep sigh of relief]. Occasionally I was in the passenger seat on family road trips typing away to shrill screaming or the singing of "Baby Shark" from the back as I composed my thoughts. No hard feelings though, as we have always been bigger proponents of our journey being unique, messy, and *ours*—an adventure with a rewarding outcome, a lot of laughter, and optimally, a big impact.

You see, success is never ever convenient. Success doesn't present itself to you in pretty Pinterest-worthy packages. More often growth is created when we have reached our own chaotic or painful tipping point, or on occasion it comes from a place of energized, blissed-out empowerment. We have experienced all of the above and know that if we can come out on the other side, then you can too.

The rewards of living the side hustle life have been worth the late nights and early mornings, food on the go, my kid's teeny tiny stickers stuck on my skirt in the meeting, the stress of patchworking babysitting schedules, finding Goldfish and Butt Paste in my handbag instead of the business materials I *actually* need, and of course the occasional, dreaded tearful good-byes!

But here's the deal—as humans, we have to *want* the adventure bad enough and have the willingness to take the mess that is our lives and have the courage to turn it into something beautiful, meaningful, and poetic.

From Us

There is something both comical and entertaining about a hyperanalytical risk analyst and world-traveling feminist finding each other, falling in love, and then building several side hustles turned full-time businesses together. We are truly the competitive type and usually with each other, and often creating a wonderful fireworks show! However, like all great business partnerships and marriages, it is our shared values, vision, drive to improve, and trust in each other's strengths that ultimately enabled us to grow our side hustles and step away from corporate life.

Having met through our mentors and joining forces, we built our first e-commerce business to over $1 million in revenue, and Carrie stepped away from her preschool teaching career in her midtwenties—creating much of the autonomy she desired. Craig continued to make progress in the corporate world, transitioning from a risk analyst role to eventually managing the growth and relationships on a loan portfolio of $100 million-plus in his twenties. While working and hustling in the evenings and on weekends, we made a choice: as we succeeded in our side hustles, Craig would continue succeeding in his job—*and we would bank the surplus income.*

We continued to grow our first business to a few million in revenue. The communication skills we developed there led to some additional coaching, teaching, public speaking, and consulting, evolving into other businesses and eclipsing Craig's banking salary. Instead of using the surplus cash to buy fancy things, we bought a couple more homes and sold them (this time profitably) and started stuffing extra cash away in the markets.

During Craig's last two years in the commercial banking industry, we saved 110 percent of his salary. We bought private equity in some firms and invested in commercial real estate deals. Some worked well, some not so well, and one downright terrible, but over time the investment portfolio grew, giving us additional security beyond our operating businesses. In 2016, we bought a new home, and the next day, we accomplished Craig's lifelong dream of stepping away from corporate life.

Many people ask us, "How did you step away from your traditional jobs in your twenties and thirties, respectively?" Our answer: *intentionally.* Our experience is most people lack real clarity on what they truly want and are often unwilling to plan, commit, and clear enough things of lesser importance out of their life.

This newfound freedom enabled us to invest more time into each other, our daughter, and add additional side hustles to our plate—along with our first nonprofit, Tandem Giving Inc., to help children in need. We also had *plenty* of time to add another child.

We now have the privilege to speak to roughly 20,000-plus people annually on several continents. Our primary focus is how to build side hustles effectively, business owner mindset, Lifeset, communication, and self empowerment. It has been an honor teaching people how to leverage entrepreneurship as a tool to create a magical life and not just make money.

We haven't done anything miraculous or ingenious. Truly we have not. We are not uber-rich and don't own any yachts or islands. I'm not sure we desire to. But most important, we are *time wealthy* and as such have been able to align much of our life and time with what we value most. In fact, we believe the biggest benefactors of our efforts have been the three- and seven-year-old humans living in our home. Customizing our time with our children, while still entrepreneuring on our terms, has fortuned us a dream life. *Perhaps the world would be a better place if more content was being produced by those who are genuinely fulfilled and happy.* A lot of content is produced by people with extraordinary talent, abilities, insane work ethic, or entrepreneurial geniuses, or who have such flawless beauty it makes the average person feel an unrelatable amount of disparity between where they are at and where the content creator is.

We do believe in learning from people at the highest levels of achievement. We admire them, respect them, and love to be challenged by them. However, while reading those narratives is oftentimes *motivational and inspiring*, it is not always *empowering.*

Most world-class athletes do not become world-class coaches. Why? Because for LeBron James to teach Craig how to dunk a basketball would be like Beethoven teaching the average toddler to play piano. It reminds us of the movie *Good Will Hunting* when Will Hunting, an extremely gifted genius, says, "I could just play." Is *that* the person you want teaching you?

Our point is, if a couple with average, middle-class backgrounds, and no extreme entrepreneurial pedigree, talent, or abilities can scale some businesses and investments to enough revenue that lets them step away from their traditional jobs—you can too. We want you to understand and believe that our side hustle success, unlike the superstars of an industry, is duplicatable and is a *real possibility* for you and your family.

So What on Earth Does This Have to Do with You?

We believe entrepreneurial desire, interest, and talent lie on a spectrum. The vast majority of people are floating in the middle; the ambiverts of entrepreneurship. They are not die-hard, risk-taking business owners, nor are they 100 percent fulfilled or secure in their full-time careers. And they know more is out there.

> People are waking up to the fact that there is less job *security* than ever, but there is also more *opportunity* than ever.

Everything we have built started out as a side hustle or still is. What we share in this book is relevant because we have lived it. It is not theoretical, statistical, or academic, but an authentic testament of our own ordinariness that we hope empowers you. People don't talk *enough* about progressive, incremental growth and just how deeply powerful a side hustle approach can be.

Aspiring side hustlers are often looking for the fast track, the easy answers on what it takes to launch and build a business successfully. Therefore, the first several chapters of this book take a more holistic, long-term view of success that so many are missing. As a result, we take a deeply foundational approach first. We want your side hustle to *enrich the quality of your life.*

Through sharing our own successes and unreserved failures, we desire to empower you to take action around your financial destiny in a way you likely haven't *yet*! We have mentored many to win and observed even more fail, and the later chapters in the book share advice for the more technical necessities of building a side hustle, like branding and raising capital. In addition, and perhaps most important, we challenge you to develop a *clear vision* for your *life* (Life Vision) and how to use a side hustle as a lever to manifest it. Without *clarity* on why you are engaging in a side hustle, it is unlikely you will see it through to something of long-lasting value.

So You Want to Start a Side Hustle is really about *you* and what brings you closer to your desired relationships, fulfillment, and lifestyle and ultimately, what matters most. We are passing on the proverbial torch and it has your name on it.

C&C (Carrie and Craig)

P.S. Please Read: What This book *Is* and *Is Not*

Before you get to the content of this book, we want you to understand what you're in for. This is *not* a book full of ideas with random things to sell or a thousand different businesses to start. There are many books for that already. Sure, we discuss some general ideas and more important, how to *evaluate business ideas and systems*, but we prefer you listen to an expert regarding whichever specific business, system, model, industry, or product you choose to build.

We have seen many people fail, not necessarily because the business, idea, or product itself was flawed, but because there were gaps in their mindset and the foundation of their life wasn't strong enough to bear the weight of building something of significance.

This book is designed as a *traveling adventure guide* for anyone who has started or wants to start a business. It can be used in tandem with your big idea, the system, franchise, real estate, or consulting business you are building.

If you are a hardcore entrepreneur requiring a deep level of venture capital investment or a slow research and development (R&D) project with years of planning, you are probably not the book's optimal audience per se. Some of the chapters will still be extremely applicable, but others may seem elementary. Use as needed.

Last, we want each of you to put our recommendations through your own filter of practicality and sense making. In a world overflowing with data points, inputs, and *mis*information, it is easy to lose your own voice or become distanced from what you truly value. We encourage you to challenge any of the advice we share (or from any source for that matter) against your own intuition and sense-making models of the universe. The thought process we used to create the life we have is by no means the *only* way to create it, nor does it need to be *your* path. We do believe you will find the majority of the recommendations helpful and supportive, but if one of the shoes doesn't fit, take it off and chuck it.

Ultimately, we aspire to empower you to *think* for yourself—because in doing so, you can *own* your thinking, a foundational skill necessary for successful business *own*ership.

ad-

A prefix indicating motion or direction to as in *advance* or reduction or change into as in *adapt*.

venture

Start a new activity, start thinking in a new way, or start doing an activity in a new place.

ad·**venture**

A daring and exciting activity calling for *enterprise* and *enthusiasm*.

dictionary.cambridge.org and google.com

CHAPTER 1

Welcome to the Side Hustle Life

Life should not be a journey to the grave with the intention of arriving safely in a pretty and well-preserved body, but rather to skid in broadside in a cloud of smoke, thoroughly used up, totally worn out, and loudly proclaiming "Wow! What a ride!"
—Hunter S. Thompson

We believe if we only get one crack, one shot at life, it is our responsibility to make it as remarkable as possible. Of course, remarkable can mean different things for different people. What does it mean to you? For us, creating a strong level of agency over our time and money has been life changing. We have achieved this lifestyle by heavily leveraging what is known as the side hustle. For people who are opposed to a lifetime of cubicle office work but don't have hardcore entrepreneurial talent or experience, the beauty and strength of a side hustle is that it can be an effective bridge to a higher level of autonomy. You can keep the stability that your regular job provides but still have the adventure, challenge, and financial rewards that come with growing your own business.

Having picked up this book, you likely look at the world of making a living very differently than most people. You have grown skeptical about job "security," making other people money, or not having agency over your own time. Frankly, you want to build something for yourself that empowers you to live your life your way.

There are, however, a large number of side hustlers really just doing gig work, never accessing the right guidance or developing a clear plan to build something that can genuinely impact their life. We don't just want to teach you how to start a side hustle, we want to teach you how to *finish* one. Meaning, we want you to build a business to a level that satisfies your personal goals and needs and truly enriches the quality of your life, not just your bank account. While consulting and mentoring others, speaking to thousands of people, and operating our own side hustles, we have seen many people win and even more fail. With the resources, technology, and community support available, our zeitgeist is shifting—requiring more people to create and take on side hustles. It is an exceptionally exciting time, and we have written this book to assist you in developing the paradigm shifts, lifestyle choices, and business strategy to keep you informed, motivated, and skilled at activating your best life through the gifts only a side hustle can offer.

> We don't just want to teach you how to start a side hustle, we want to teach you how to *finish* one.

So What the Heck Is a Side Hustle Anyway?

The business lexicon is ever changing, ever evolving, and when it comes to the term *side hustle*, it is rather elusive. Not found in *Webster's* dictionary (yet), although to its credit, the site lists the term under "words we're watching."

Dictionary.com, on the other hand, has taken a stab at a definition in its slang section:

> *Side hustle* is a means of making money alongside one's main form of employment or income. The term *side hustle* took off in the 2000s thanks to two forces: the internet and the gig economy. The internet allowed people to earn money through projects on social media, such as making money on blogs or selling crafts on Etsy. The gig economy, like driving Uber or freelancing on Fiverr, allowed people more opportunities for a *side hustle* outside their main income.

There is often confusion about the difference between a side hustle and a gig. Gig work is generally temporary and limited in both income and effort. It has an expiration date. Think modern-day "shift worker." A side hustle is ever-evolving and represents something that is designed to be built for an extended period of time and can be scaled into a business that can replace an individual's primary line of work or even eventually grow into a large corporation.

Our personal definition of side hustle is more conceptual and indicative of a *movement* than simply a trendy-sounding adjective or noun. After all, the side hustle has become intertwined with our economy, our sense of personal fulfillment, our stability, and even our personal branding, so reducing the term to just something that you do seems to be misaligned with the shifts of twenty-first-century reality. We are no longer in the world of industrial-age job security, loyalty to one company for a lifetime, and guaranteed pensions. We live in an economy with less job security than ever before, but we have even more opportunity than ever before. The internet, social media, and technology in general have made it more affordable and accessible for the average person to start a business. Why not diversify by using a moderate, practical approach: keep the day job for your stable income, to pay the bills and save for the future, all while building a side hustle for your variable income.

While there are many courses and certifications on entrepreneurship and how to build a business, we have yet to discover any curricula or guidance from the trenches on how to become a successful entrepreneur *while holding on to the 9-to-5* and how to synergize that side hustle with building a high-caliber life. That is our objective here—to give you a much-needed window of insight so you have the tools to make your hustle take flight.

What Stage of the Side Hustle Are You In?

Because we firmly believe that side hustles turn into lifestyles, and that the level to which you side hustle can impact the quality and style of your life, the guidance throughout this book fits every stage of the game. Whether you know you need to build something for yourself but have no idea what or where to start, have been told your talent can be monetized (or should be) but don't have a clue how, or are side hustling already and desire to level up, your next steps are all about introspection and strategy—and this book is chock-full of both. This book offers the fundamentals for determining the Life Vision that drives your side hustle, WHO to start associating with, WHAT to choose as a vehicle, and HOW to execute so you can ultimately create the life you want.

Common Side Hustle Scenarios

What is so infectious about side hustling in general is how eclectic our economy has become. We often run into the following common scenarios when coaching aspiring side hustlers, illustrating a range of strengths, obstacles, and uniqueness in their journeys. If you've already started the process of building a side hustle or thought about it, you can likely relate to aspects of these examples.

The Artist

I am talented, passionate, and independent. I have a product or service that people appreciate and will spend good money on. I am the photographer, the woodworker, the painter, the refurbishing expert, the interior designer, or the vlogger. Despite my skills, I often lack strong business experience or expertise. I also struggle to have a strategy for growth, manage the business financials, or stay on top of my deliverables. I don't necessarily take myself all that seriously (yet) and frequently give my services away for free to friends and family (or in exchange for dinners and beer). I have talent that benefits others, but I need more support, structure, accountability, and guidance in treating my side hustle like a real viable business—so I can make it one.

The Consultant

I have invaluable assets called experience and a clear expertise. I know how to deliver and get things done in my particular industry. My wisdom has helped me grow and succeed in the corporate world or gig economy, but I am unclear how to take my game to the next level and replace my full-time income. I do well in my career, so there is significant income that needs to be generated; making a transition out of my job feels difficult to accomplish.

The Network Marketer

I have a deep desire to grow, change, and be part of a supportive community while I'm in the pursuit. I am open minded and an achiever, but I don't have a lot of capital and am not in a position to assume a lot of risk.

I am willing to play off of existing systems and don't necessarily have to be creating a business from scratch, but I am just as much an entrepreneur as the next in my initiative and willingness to learn and develop if I find the right environment to perform and can stay patient.

The Aspiring Real Estate Investor

I am aspirational and have a strong vision. I like to take risks and am a big-picture thinker. I love the idea of being able to invest and create ongoing income streams, but I lack either the capital, expertise, or clarity on how to reverse engineer a practical plan and get there in reality. I often struggle to take action to back up my ideas. I need more guidance to know what the next step is, otherwise I tend to talk a big game and not walk the walk.

Whichever of these you most closely align with, get ready to make your situation monetizable. But this will not happen without your making a few life adjustments and setting new and clear priorities. In the event you are still on the fence, our persuasive argument for dipping more than just your one big toe in the ocean of side hustling follows.

Fun Facts: Side Hustles That Became Cultural Icons

- FedEx was created by the owner of Arkansas Aviation Sales.
- Nike was started by an accountant.
- Twitter got its start by a web developer.
- Spanx was founded by a fax machine salesperson.
- Google was launched by two PhD students.
- Under Armour was started by a college football player.
- Craigslist was created by a computer programmer.
- Apple was born while Steve Jobs and Steve Wozniak had jobs at Atari and Hewlett Packard.
- Facebook was launched by college students.
- Udemy was founded by an Accenture consultant.

And the list could go on and on . . .

Eight Reasons to Start *and* Prioritize a Side Hustle

It's one thing to start a business, but the biggest rewards and benefits of building a side hustle come from *actually* building it. For many, it's not the initial honeymoon excitement that presents the challenge; it's the follow-through. It's the lack of conviction and true commitment that it takes to build something substantial.

> **The reason most people fail in building a side hustle is because they treat it like one.**

The following list gives reasons why we encourage you to dig your heels in and fully embrace the side hustle movement for the long haul.

1. Diversifying in the Twenty-First Century Should Be Nonoptional

People say starting a business is risky. We believe going through life with only one way to make money is risky, and having only one way to make money in the twenty-first century is arguably irresponsible.

Have you *ever* met a financial planner who advised you to put all your money into just one stock? The answer is an emphatic no, so why put all your eggs into one basket when it comes to your *income*?

Also, asking your full-time job to fulfill *all* your financial needs and career development is like expecting your life partner to complete all your emotional needs. You have relationships in your life *outside* your spouse for a reason. Remember: one of the only guarantees with a job is that someday you will not have it!

> **We believe going through life with only one way to make money is risky, and having only one way to make money in the twenty-first century is arguably irresponsible.**

2. Building a Side Hustle Can Create More Time for Your Future Self

Once we learned about the concept of building assets that can create passive or ongoing revenue, our mindset completely shifted. What are you doing or building today to create more time, security, and peace of mind for yourself in the future? Building our side hustles large enough to replace our 9-to-5 jobs required additional time investment up front for several years, but it has been infinitely worth the rewards. We didn't want time to be our excuse for not building our side hustles, so time became the *reason* we built them.

3. Developing New Skills Is Critical for Your Financial Security

Acquiring new skills is one of the most paramount things you can do for your financial future and can play a major role in your happiness. For most people, the first few years in their new careers can provide a big learning curve. However, even with a promotion or two, the learning curve tends to dissipate. It's not that you aren't learning; it's that you typically aren't learning as much, and oftentimes the subject matter or expertise narrows. The drawback with most jobs is they can't challenge you in *all* the ways you want to be challenged. Building a side hustle pushes you out of your comfort zone and has you developing new skills that you wouldn't otherwise.

For instance, when Craig was working as a risk analyst, there was not exactly an abundance of public-speaking opportunities, and he always labeled himself as more of an analytic than a sales guy or public speaker. However, building a side hustle forced him to start developing these skills, which in turn transferred into his career, allowing him to move into business development, doubling his job income. These skills boosted his public-speaking career, a passion and ability Craig would have never developed if he had just been crunching numbers in corporate America. This mindset and momentum around skill development still continues to this day, and so have the benefits.

4. You Enhance Your Financial Education and Your Understanding of How Taxes Work

Most people are taught language, academic, or job literacy, but they are not required to attend classes on *financial literacy*, which hones a deeper understanding and application of budgeting, investing, and overall personal financial management.

Learning how the tax code works and how you can leverage it *in your favor* is a game changer for most side hustlers. Even if you don't make a dime from your side hustle and run at a small loss for a few years with a home-based business, the amount of education and deductions you can capture is of value and may offset any manageable losses. Use a side hustle to break free of being intimidated by the tax code and learn how to use it to your advantage.

5. A Side Hustle Forces You to Grow Your Entrepreneurial Network, Enhancing Your Leverage

We can attest to your network equating to your net worth. We wouldn't say it's exactly a 1-to-1 ratio, but there is a huge correlation. Think about it, how did you find your first job? If you are going to find another one, how would you start? Imagine the value of building out your network into new industries, arenas, or spheres of influence. A side hustle challenges you to put yourself in front of people you wouldn't otherwise. If you do quality work and develop authentic relationships, it amplifies your network and influence. Developing your networking skills is crucial, and many job roles never provide an opportunity to do this, or if so, only in a limited industry-specific capacity.

6. A Side Hustle Can Be a Life Raft During Economic Changes and Disruptions

The need to navigate the exponential growth of technology, artificial intelligence, and other economic uncertainties is more certain than ever. It's paramount that you challenge the way you think and be realistic about the impact technology has already had on the way we work—eliminating positions as well as creating entirely new industries. Because of things like tech and AI, you cannot count on the continued existence of your domain or industry, or your function within them.

Planning now for what might be inevitable will help you avoid getting stuck as a "specialist," clinging to a skill or industry that might soon be obsolete, or one that already is. Building your side hustle will help you become more dynamic when it comes to finding work in the future.

7. Building a Side Hustle Develops Your Personal Brand

Your personal personal brand now carries more magnitude than ever before. Back in the dark ages (the 1980s) there were only a handful of major television channels, radio stations, and so on. Now we have thousands of different ways to market not only a company but *you*. You, as a brand.inc already exists. The only question is what does that brand sound, feel, and look like? So how does having a side hustle help? *We believe entrepreneurship is one of the best forms of self-development.* When people begin to think of you as someone who is growth oriented and willing to improve themselves, they have a harder time putting you in a box! If you do this through honesty and good, quality work, your branding improves. In addition, you can always take your brand with you, even when you leave a job, company, or industry. It's an asset, and we recommend taking it seriously. We discuss personal branding in greater detail in Chapters 6 and 11.

8. For the Adventure and the Love of the Game

If you are reading this book, you may be craving some additional adventure in your life. There is likely a desire for another challenge or a new experience, or at least to have a chance at a financial home run (also giving you the thrill of possible failure). Everyone *craves these things*; it's just in the intensity, frequency, and duration of the adventure that people might differ. Starting your side hustle *definitely* gives you a renewed sense of excitement in your life. Don't you want to grow and do things that make you feel alive?

Note: We are *not* advising you to start performing poorly as an employee! On the contrary, we recommend applying the skills you learn from your side hustle and bringing them *to* your job—and vice versa. Most companies want you to engage in self-development and often pay for you to attend formal training programs. By challenging yourself to run your own company in your "off hours," you naturally develop newfound skills and confidence. If you bring this into your work environment, coupled with a humble attitude, you will shine. We have witnessed this unfold with scores of individuals we have personally coached and mentored.

How to Identify If Side Hustling Is *Not* Your Thing

We often see people revved up and ready to go with starting a side hustle, but there are some key parameters that should be considered in an effort to qualify yourself and your own ambitions. This way you can be certain a side hustle is, in fact, the right play and the correct area of investment before going too far down the path. Timing matters, and a side hustle certainly isn't for everyone!

1. **You are already content.** If you are fully content with your current sources of income because they provide you the amount of income, flexibility, personal growth, and security you desire, there is no need to hustle beyond that. If anything, you can enjoy the fruits of your current labors or give back through charitable efforts or income. However, it's unlikely you would've picked up this book if you are feeling *fully satisfied* in all these buckets.

2. **Leisure time is your priority.** You are unwilling or unable to work evenings and weekends. *Hustle* is the operative word. There is additional work to be done, and if you already work traditional hours, then after hours are what's left over to build a business. If you're not up for that type of sweat equity, then a side hustle is probably not an ideal approach for you.

3. **You have mismanaged expectations.** Many people are poking side hustles with a stick but expecting to create significant outcomes. There's a disconnect between what they want to create and what they are actually creating. Someone might be stuck thinking or planning, which can be emotionally tolling. *Thinking* about building something often misleads people into believing they are building it.

   An epidemic with some side hustlers is they tend to hop from project to project when they don't see immediate results. Building a legitimate business takes time and a lot of patience. It's important to have realistic expectations about how much money you are going to make or how much work it's going to take to be profitable. We don't define side hustling as a get-rich-quick option; it's about building something real, requiring real effort.

4. **You are eyeing up a front hustle.** You want to go full-throttle business owner *yesterday*. Are you ready to burn the ships and fight to the end? Please see our next section.

Why a Side Hustle and *Not* a Front Hustle

If you want your business to be a priority, why not go full time? Or what if you have a deep burning passion to run a restaurant and it necessitates going "all in"? If you are asking these questions, to be completely honest, you *might* be right. We agree, there is a chance you may need to take the big plunge, leave the day job, and push all the chips across the table. For some, that larger leap of faith or added pressure may be necessary. Just make sure you truly understand yourself and the risks involved. If that's the case—go for it.

However, for the *extreme vast* majority, we call bullsh** on the "all in or all out" attitude and recommend you stop processing decisions with a fixed binary mindset. Using statements such as, "I do something either 100 percent or not at all" is fallible. Have you ever had a girlfriend *and* gone to college? Had a child *and* still had a social life? Had a job *and* a hobby? Are you giving 100 percent to your girlfriend, child, or career all at the same time? Nope.

So instead of a binary thought process, let's work together to operate *in reality*. We have asked the following list of questions to friends or mentees who were looking to go "all in" on a restaurant. We challenged them to keep their jobs and instead consider the following side hustles: What about . . .

- ▶ Starting a food cart?
- ▶ Launching a catering business?
- ▶ Cooking high-end meals for private parties?
- ▶ Donating your time to cook great meals for underprivileged children or individuals spending their last days in hospice?
- ▶ Offering to work for a highly regarded local chef for *free* so you can learn the trade first?

We suggest our mentees use the previous options to create a brand or micro-brand for themselves, raise some extra capital, confirm they indeed do love the work, do additional research, and *then* invest a few hundred thousand dollars to start a restaurant and quit the day job. If you think you are ready to be a big league, full-time entrepreneur but have never sold a product or service, here are some additional questions to ask yourself:

- ▸ Can you make a couple of sales first?
- ▸ Can you pilot a side hustle experience by picking up a client or two?
- ▸ Is the work or business harder than you thought?
- ▸ Do you love the work so much you are willing to spend many of your waking hours doing it?
- ▸ Do you love the technical work but loathe marketing and networking? Is that something you are willing to push through, or should you consider getting a partner or outsourcing some of those tasks to a marketing firm or intern?

The preceding type of activity provides confirmation you do in fact like the work associated with the side hustle and that you are willing to do it for long enough to see results, even on a small level!

It is our humble opinion that for most, there is more to gain by starting with a side hustle than there is to lose. You can be the practical Clark Kent news reporter during the day—then rip off the suit and go do your superhero thing in the evening.

Remember, *your job* might actually be a vehicle for you to learn new skills, develop a network, build confidence, and grow deep expertise in a particular subject matter and raise basic seed money to fund your side hustle. Of course, we were thankful for the jobs we had when we had them. For the record though, we are even more thankful those jobs are no longer a necessity.

> **You can be the practical Clark Kent news reporter during the day—then rip off the suit and go do your superhero thing in the evening.**

If you manage your finances well, the surplus cash from your job income can provide the venture capital for your side hustle. This does *many* powerful things. It allows your side hustle to run in a sustainable way (even at a loss) for *years*, if necessary. This empowers you to do things for your business you know are *right*, not necessarily for short-term cash or commission. You can play the long game. We have seen plenty of real estate agents or financial advisors over the years do and sell things for short-term money at the cost of long-term profit, reputation—or worse, at the cost of their clients or values. Many companies do not survive, not for lack of enthusiasm or a good idea, but due to a lack of *funding*. A lot of entrepreneurs who are always in need of funding are forced to spend excessive amounts of mental and physical energy raising it. We were personally more energized to operate and grow our businesses versus constantly asking others for money to fund it.

Finally, and most important, if you have a clear plan, acquire a mentor, find a community to support you, and manage your expectations. We believe that for most people, running a side hustle carries lower stress levels than quitting your job and working to build something from scratch full time with your bare hands—or borrowing a lot of money.

The Scalability Bias

We reference the idea of scaling (F/K/A "growing") your side hustle frequently throughout this book. Our assumption is that most people who build out a business want to effectively grow it to the next level. We are biased as our end goal was to build enough ongoing revenue to replace our regular jobs *and* create a low-stress and flexible lifestyle. However, this doesn't *have* to be the case for you. There are plenty of people in the world who love their craft or trade and are completely content keeping their growth low key and informal. If you're part of the latter population, there is still ample mindset that's beneficial to you—but implement what is helpful for your goals and pacing.

At this point, you might be thinking "Got it C&C, but *what* the heck do I do to get moving?" We're getting there, but before we do, we need you to ask yourself some more probing questions. We need you to step outside your body and have some meta conversations. WHY do *you* want to build a side hustle? We advise you develop some real clarity around what you are looking to create. Otherwise, when the going gets tough (and it always does), you will end up like most side hustlers, lost in the black hole of great ideas or the infinite abyss of good intentions.

We don't want you to start a side adventure that someday turns into *"that"* project" collecting dust in the corner of your basement, garage, or office. The kind that every time you or your spouse walks by, is a painful reminder of one more "thing" you didn't follow through on, or worse, have failed at. We have no intention of fostering that type of hit to your ego, self-image, or happiness. You need to have your mindset and Lifeset ready for success, so you can dictate *where* the heck you are going. This helps you harness the energy required to keep you on point and turn your side adventure into something meaningful.

Now that you know what a side hustle is, you have to consider it in the context of the results you want to create, which we call your Life Vision. When you start dialing into your desired outcomes, you can narrow in your focus with the clarity and conviction necessary to generate them over time. As a side hustler, you are the driver. You have the keys and a full tank of gas, but you do need to identify your destination and punch it into the GPS, which is the central focus of the next chapter.

CHAPTER 2

Developing Your Life Vision

Having a vision for your life allows you to live out of hope, rather than out of your fears.
—Stedman Graham

When considering a side hustle, or even a profession for that matter, most people go straight to the WHAT: what is their product, what is their service, or what is their skill. No doubt, the product or service is the vehicle and we agree this is important; in fact, we wrote an entire chapter on the WHAT, but it isn't your *first* stop. We propose a paradigm shift by, as Stephen Covey famously suggested, "beginning with the end in mind." In other words, begin with your vision. How do you want to live? What type of person do you want to become? What are your core values? What is important to you? Your answers to these questions (your WHY or many WHYs) help you build out your Life Vision. This Life Vision, among many things, provides a framework, metrics, and targets. Your side hustle can now become a tool, a vehicle, to accomplish those targets.

A Life Vision is like a GPS. When you need directions to go somewhere, what do you populate into your GPS? *A specific address.* However, when most people get in their vehicle called life, they enter vague destinations such as "I want to be fulfilled," or "I want to help people." There is nothing wrong with either, but if you put "south" into your GPS and end up in the desert wishing it was Disney World, the problem was not "WHAT" mode of transportation you used. Blaming life for not ending up where you want, when you haven't defined the result, the destination you'd like to arrive at, is not your life's fault either.

Your Life Vision provides you a target, something you can begin to develop real, tangible goals around. We started side hustling for many reasons, a big one being that we knew our Life Vision (result) included financial autonomy and to step away from our 9-to-5 jobs. We laid out very clear parameters on how to create that outcome for ourselves.

We know a successful accountant who wanted to step away from her career to spend more time with her children and do volunteer work. She built up her side hustle as a real estate agent, putting concrete goals together for how many clients she would need to service and what that would equate to in terms of net profit. Over time she was able to make that transition, which fed into her Life Vision of additional time with her family and her nonprofit work.

A family friend of ours was a successful marketing manager who also has a passion for public speaking. His Life Vision was anchored in keeping his full-time profession but also book enough public-speaking opportunities on an annual basis that he would gain the fulfillment and impact he felt was missing from his 9-to-5 as well as provide a financial target to help support his parent's monthly assisted living expenses. He has been very clear on what the frequency of his speaking engagements should be in order to achieve his desired life outcome.

Developing a clear Life Vision facilitates goal setting with great specificity; when your goals are more measurable, they become more achievable and iterative. You can also better understand how these goals fit into your overall picture.

So what is your Life Vision and how does building a business assist you in creating or supporting that vision? Although in the last chapter we discussed many reasons a side hustle makes sense, the journey of entrepreneurship is one of intentionality, and it requires *your* reasons, not just *some* reasons. These are not just rhetorical or theoretical questions. They are actual questions and some of the most paramount. If you don't have clear answers, why not? It is alarming how many people have never answered these questions for themselves, and what's even more fascinating is how no one has likely ever asked them.

Step 1: Start *Now!*

If you don't start defining your Life Vision *now* there is a good chance you never will.

It is imperative to start the process of identifying your Life Vision even when you don't have every piece of the puzzle in your hands. That may feel overwhelming at first, but know that the longer you take to begin the process, the less time you have to manifest it. Also, your Life Vision and goals are not fixed but are ever evolving, so you can always make changes as you discover new things you would like to add. Embracing that we didn't need to stick the perfect landing on our first try gave us the freedom to take the first step.

Carrie here. As a senior in college, I was backpacking around India and vividly remember being at Mahatma Gandhi's cremation site. The bold words "My Life Is My Message" hung on the wall. The iconic phrase took on new depth in that moment and really challenged me to look in the mirror and figure out what I wanted my livelihood, my pursuit, and my impact to look like. This set me on a path of evaluating my trajectory and thinking about what I wanted my Life Vision to be.

As I solidified plans and goals around that vision, I was drawn to entrepreneurship, not only for the monetary rewards, but as a tool to customize my time with my family and long-term impact like starting a nonprofit. I didn't have my entire life mapped out, but I realized that relying on a 9-to-5 job would not be enough to get me the results I wanted. Beginning to work on my Life Vision helped me confirm these decisions, identify my anchoring values, and begin to build a real plan.

Let me be clear, you don't have to go to the foothills of the Himalayas to have these breakthroughs, but you do need to dedicate the time. Give yourself the gift of starting the process—and the time and space to authentically explore how you want to live and what you want to create.

Waiting to work on your vision will do you no favors. So *now*, at a very high level lets do some prelimary work, and as a brainstorming process to get the momentum flowing (before we get more specific), list five desirable characteristics of your life 10 years from now.

1. _____

2. _____

3. _____

4. _____

5. _____

Step 2: Establish Your Values

As you begin to think about your future and how you want to live, it should give you some solid insight into what you value. Establishing your top values also helps align your Life Vision, ensuring you don't just randomly put up ideas that sound fun or cute, without cross-referencing what is truly meaningful to you.

In discerning your top values, we suggest taking a look at the following list of values. Invest some time now thinking about which you connect with. Many books recommend choosing your top three to five values. We each have five of our own personally. For our company, Tandem Consulting, we chose our top three: family, adventure, impact. Of course, you likely have many more values that resonate with you, but your core values should be very specific. In fact, having more than five primary core values may actually dilute the ones that matter the most, so zoom in on the ones that stand above all others.

Many of the words in the following list may have similar meanings, but some will resonate with you better. For example, Craig has oscillated between *honesty* and *integrity* on his top five list . . . but went with *integrity* because it felt more all-encompassing than the word *honesty*. Carrie is a strong proponent of *fun*, but ultimately chose *adventure*, as that value encapsulates fun but better captures the risks and rewards of the entrepreneurial journey.

Let's begin now by selecting some words and values that speak to you. Note, people's environments and associations have often left such deep imprinting that many have never truly stepped back and identified these values for themselves. Give yourself the benefit of claiming your own values.

Highlight *all* of the words that really connect for you as you read this list.

Abundance	Commitment	Excellence	Industrious
Acceptance	Communication	Exploration	Innovation
Accountability	Compassion	Expressiveness	Inspiration
Achievement	Connection	Fairness	Integrity
Advancement	Cooperation	Faith	Intelligence
Adventure	Collaboration	Family	Intuition
Advocacy	Consistency	Fitness	Joy
Ambition	Contribution	Flexibility	Justice
Appreciation	Creativity	Fortitude	Kindness
Assertiveness	Credibility	Freedom	Knowledge
Attractiveness	Curiosity	Friendships	Leadership
Autonomy	Daring	Fun	Learning
Balance	Decisiveness	Generosity	Liberty
Being the Best	Dedication	Grace	Love
Benevolence	Dependability	Gratitude	Loyalty
Boldness	Determination	Greatness	Making a Difference
Bravery	Dignity	Growth	
Brilliance	Discovery	Happiness	Mindfulness
Calmness	Diversity	Harmony	Motivation
Caring	Drive	Health	Optimism
Challenge	Earnestness	Honesty	Open-Mindedness
Charity	Empathy	Honor	
Clarity	Encouragement	Humility	Orderly
Challenging	Endurance	Humor	Originality
Charisma	Enjoyment	Impact	Passion
Cheerfulness	Enthusiasm	Inclusiveness	Performance
Cleverness	Empowerment	Independence	Personal Development
Community	Ethics	Individuality	

Poise	Reliability	Sincerity	Uniqueness
Proactive	Resilience	Solitude	Unity
Professionalism	Resourcefulness	Speed	Usefulness
Peace	Respect	Spirituality	Versatility
Perfection	Responsibility	Spontaneous	Victory
Playfulness	Responsiveness	Stability	Vision
Popularity	Risk Taking	Status	Vitality
Power	Safety	Success	Warmth
Preparedness	Security	Teamwork	Wealth
Proactivity	Self-Control	Thankfulness	Well-Being
Professionalism	Selflessness	Thoughtfulness	Wisdom
Punctuality	Sensual	Timeliness	Wonder
Quality	Serenity	Traditionalism	Zeal
Realistic	Service	Trustworthiness	
Recognition	Sexual	Truthful	
Relationships	Simplicity	Understanding	

Then use the following space to narrow that list down to your top five.

1. _____

2. _____

3. _____

4. _____

5. _____

Now that you've established your personal values, these words can help drive and guide building out your Life Vision. In addition, these values can be pulled into many other aspects of your life, from how you invest your time and planning out your schedule to making small or major decisions in your day-to-day life. When we have had different challenges come up in our life, these values have helped provide a sense of clarity and peace. We can't always control the results in our life, but if we live by our values, we can sleep well at night knowing we anchored ourselves in our personal ethics.

Step 3: Identify Your Current Phase of Life—and Where You Want to Go Next!

The best chess players, pool players, entrepreneurs, and athletes are skilled at anticipating events *before* they happen. They can often visualize and predict further and more accurately into the future than their peers. Why not work to visualize and approach your life in the same way?

Due to the scope and magnitude of creating a clear Life Vision, we decided to divide our life into six different phases. By knowing what phase of life we are currently in, we have a reference point to then peer deeper into the next phase and meditate on where we want to be and what type of person we want to become.

Society tends to categorize life into childhood, young adult, adult, and retired/senior. We decided to be more specific and create two extra phases, which enabled us to break down our goals and vision for each phase in a more manageable way.

Embracing that life will have different phases has provided an elevated peace of mind and oftentimes higher level of acceptance while buried deep into our current phase. For example, having small children and *constantly* changing diapers or loading and unloading car seats in and out of minivans is more manageable knowing we won't have the "opportunity" to do these activities *forever*; it is simply a part of life's phase 3, and it will pass.

> **When you remember that each of the Life Phases are finite, you can develop a deeper sense of appreciation and gratitude for life's journey and the phase you are in.**

Six Life Phases

A breakdown of these phases and brief description for each follows. We refrained from adding more standard age sets, as obviously, elements of all of life's different phases intertwine with each other. Many people traverse these phases at different speeds or may skip some altogether, and they are fluid as people change, evolve, or pivot in life. But from a macro level, this framework has provided us stronger reference points in designing a Life Vision and ultimately a life we are energized to both *pursue and live.*

1. **Learning:** Childhood, school, and becoming our own person
2. **Exploring:** Beginning adult life, starting a profession, traveling, dating, and meeting new people; expanding our experiences
3. **Professional:** Becoming an expert in our profession, getting married, building a family
4. **Leadership:** Leading in our career, raising and assisting other individuals, children, or organizations through phases 2 and 3
5. **Enjoyment:** Enjoying the rewards of our labor, time with grandchildren, giving, traveling, hobbies, deepening our relationships and our faith.
6. **Departing:** Preparing for our final days

Although it may be difficult to determine exactly where you want to be in phase 5 when you are still in phase 2, you can more clearly know and define where you want to be at the end of your current phase, or the beginning or well into your next phase. A 5- or 10-year Life Vision often aligns with this time horizon. For example, asking ourselves how we wanted our lives to look at age 35 when we were 16 would have been nearly impossible, but at 27, this becomes not only manageable, but extremely valuable.

Although there is value in establishing a Life Vision for each phase, for the purpose of this book we focus on developing your 5- and *10-year Life Vision.* Although human beings can make a lot of changes in a year, it is difficult to make a radical shift in your financial lifestyle, personality, confidence, deeper belief systems, or to build a business to a level of financial independence in such a short period. Five and ten years are often close enough you can visualize, but far enough you can still make significant progress. Many people are too naive on how little impact you can create in a year but how much *exponential impact* you can create in a decade.

In terms of finances, another reason we choose to focus on 5 and 10 years is because of common business trajectories we have observed. A generic timeline we have seen in our own businesses and hundreds more with Craig's background as a business and commercial banker follows. Keep in mind, by retaining the security of a job, you are likely investing less time than someone who has started a business for their full-time career, which may lengthen the time to create results.

The Standard Timeline and Trajectory of the Side Hustle

Year 1: You don't really know what you are doing. You have to learn some new skills (if you have a background in sales, you likely have to learn some bookkeeping or organizational skills). You may find a few clients. You may make some money, but you are not exactly sure what to charge or how to bill them, or you may undercharge. Maybe your product takes longer to produce. You burn too much time on things like getting your EIN number, your logo, branding, your social media accounts, your websites, seminars, licensing, legal conversations, state unemployment taxes, sales tax, and so on.

Years 2–3: You have a few things figured out. You have some sense of rhythm. Some people who doubted you now believe you are serious (booyah!). However, doubt and disbelief *will* arrive at some point. Year 1, 2, or 3, it will come. You also become a bit tired of the monotony and redundancy of the work. Some clients love you and others post negative experiences on Reddit or Facebook or make harsh comments on your Yelp profile.

Years 3–5: You get things rolling! You start to feel some real progress. You begin to make some money. But you also have days of being whacked with redundancy. Your side hustle work is no longer novel. Likely, a competitor comes along. Maybe you have a business partner or hire an employee or contractor (oftentimes a friend or family member), and it doesn't work out well. A vendor or platform you use potentially changes. But things are moving.

Years 6–7: You have learned how to survive and be profitable. Maybe you make a solid professional income. You have some contractors or employees, one or two leave, but you can manage. You have worked hard, but at least you are being compensated for the fruits of your labor. But in many ways the business has consumed you. You have worked *ultrahard*, and looking back you often wonder if it has been worth it. There have been many sacrifices, such as time with family or friends or leisure. But although you have sacrificed much, you are willing to keep pushing.

Years 8–9: You have assembled a quality team and weeded out some of the bad apples. You have great clients who now provide you consistent referrals. You have trained staff who *can handle situations without you*—hell yeah! You can take vacations and still make money. You get more time with your family than the average person who has a traditional 9-to-5 job, and you ultimately have more choices.

Year 10+: Exponential growth kicks in. You have created wealth. You have a lifestyle where you were initially underpaid and worked like a dog for years but you now feel overpaid. There are still challenges, still fires to put out, but not the mundane ones. You have built a real business, and you have the flexibility in your life that most desire or only dream of. If you have been true to the other values of your Life Vision, your side hustle has now transpired into a life that has in many ways exceeded your expectations.

Now, this timeline is general and nonindustry specific. Obviously, if you are starting a bookkeeping side hustle, the trajectory looks much different than an electric car company or an organic apple orchard. However, an amazing lifestyle doesn't occur at the onset of your adventure. For most it occurs after *years* in the game. Of course, you can make money earlier, but if your goal is to create passive income and assets, then building systems and hiring and training employees and contractors is a *much* different animal.

It goes without saying there are exceptions. We have seen and met them! But they are *rare*. The proprietors are usually entrepreneurial geniuses, extremely lucky, or both. It's critical to have enough self-awareness combined with the right amount of optimism, analytics, and market dynamics if you are going to bank your Life Vision on blowing by a more standardized timeline. However, when you have a clear expectation on where you are going, *why* you are going there, and a realistic timeline, your chances of success radically improve. Understanding this timeline helps you more realistically set goals for your business and see how those goals couple with your Life Vision. Consider which of the previous phases of life you are in currently, as we take a closer look at characteristics and parameters you would like to create into your next phase.

Once, Craig was working with a brewery that his bank was serenading to become a client. They had bought several acres of land, built a huge facility, and had their brewing equipment in one small corner. When asked why the facility was so large (they needed only a fraction of the floor space), the owner provided a logistical breakdown of the firm's 10-year goals and the facility was built by reverse engineering a plan from that vision. In fact, they had purchased state-of-the-art equipment (unnecessary for a brewery of that size) to minimize growing pains years down the road. It was *science* in the owner's mind and was also extremely impressive. Most entrepreneurs launching companies do not think this far ahead, let alone execute a real plan to manifest it. Now imagine the magnitude of doing this for your life, not just a business.

Step 4: Develop a Holistic Life Vision

When thinking about your Life Vision, people have a propensity to jump immediately and exclusively to their income, career, or business goals. Realize that your financial goals and being a side hustler are just a portion of that vision. Your vision should include all the major components of life. We cannot begin to share with you how many entrepreneurs we know who have won big in business but ended up losing in their marriage, health, or other key components of their life. What is the point of being a hotshot entrepreneur if you have low-quality relationships, are in poor health, or struggle to be truly fulfilled? This is a common trap and why it is so critical you know why you want to build a side hustle to begin with and how it synergizes with your larger Life Vision.

We need to decide how our side hustle affects, enhances, and influences all aspects of our lives, the major ones being:

- Spiritual
- Financial
- Relationships
- Health
- Recreation

By combining these aspects of your life into a *single vision*, you are less likely to create success in one area and become negligent in others. As much as people like to compartmentalize these into individual silos, they are interconnected. The health of one affects the health of another.

Every year, the president of the United States addresses the nation and delivers a State of the Union Address. We equate your Life Vision to something similar. What would you like your future "State of the Human" address to sound like? The "State of Craig or Carrie" address would include not just how much money we make or have, but our overall *state of being*. We have also heard this referred to as your *desired future state* or *future desired state*. What does happiness look and *feel* like? What would you want to have accomplished? How would you visualize your relationships at an optimal level? What are you known for? How do you want to live? How can you better act in alignment with your values?

> **Note:** "Achievement" doesn't have to be your driving force in life to be happy. Knowing yourself, your capabilities, and discovering what is true north for your own internal compass is important work. There is a good chance if you are reading this book that you may be prone to measuring your life by achievements and consider yourself a driven or success-minded person. One of our main goals is to get to our final stage of life having *fully lived and without regrets.* Whatever your Life Vision includes, make sure it is *honest*, and make sure it is *yours.*
>
> A successful entrepreneur we know shared an insightful story with us. One day his janitor professed he would likely be a janitor his whole life. He didn't mind that but realized if he was going to be a janitor, instead of doing so in a small town in Wisconsin, he could be a janitor in *Hawaii.* Several months later, he moved to Hawaii, found a janitorial job, and would occasionally send a postcard explaining how great life was on the island.
>
> How we define success is ours to author.

Most people have never been pushed to engage in activity as comprehensive or holistic as building out a Life Vision. As a result, they often perform poorly and come back with very vague statements or goals such as:

- ▶ "I want to be financially independent."
- ▶ "I want to have a lot of flexibility to travel."
- ▶ "I want to have a great relationship with my husband."
- ▶ "I want to help my parents."

These are weak sauce goals at best; they are too surface level. Better than *no* goals, but not by much. Your vision and goals need to be *specific* and provide clarity in your life. Being too vague, overarching, or theoretical on goals is a great way to never accomplish them. Deeper purpose and cause are important; they provide fuel, and you want to anchor your action plan around them. Remember the five characteristics about your future life we had you share in the last section? This is about as deep as most people ever go, and as a result, they never develop a clear plan. It's impossible to execute on a plan that doesn't exist.

Hundreds of books have been written on goal setting, but for the purpose of our conversation we recommend that each of the five categories of your vision include the following:

1. Quantifiable metrics with dates (for those items that allow)
2. Activity goals
3. Values, characteristics, feelings, or visuals that express your desired future state

As an example, it may be hard to have a quantifiable spiritual goal. What we can recommend is to have an *activity* goal. The following examples are deeper and more specific:

1. **Original Goal:** "I want to be financially independent."
   Specific Goal: "I want to achieve financial independence by age 40." This requires:

   - ▶ $60,000 of annual passive income from at least two different sources (metric)
   - ▶ $500,000 in total savings, 401(k), or other (metric)
   - ▶ No major financial commitments or debt and home paid off in full (metric)
   - ▶ Carry a strong feeling of financial security (feeling)

2. **Original Goal:** "I want to have a lot of flexibility to travel."
   Specific Goal: "I want to be able to travel four months out of the year by 2024."

   ▸ Need a work-from-home career or six-to-eight month project/contract work (metric)
   ▸ Have a partner who values traveling and does not want to own a home or have children for several years (metric)
   ▸ Need $20,000 in liquid savings (metric)
   ▸ Want the feeling of not being tied down or restricted (feeling)

3. **Original Goal:** "I want to have a great relationship with my husband."
   Specific Goal: "I want to have a marriage I love and that I am actively investing time and work into."

   ▸ Attend annual marriage retreats (activity)
   ▸ Volunteer together as a weekly activity (activity)
   ▸ Invest at least one weekend a month just for us (activity)
   ▸ We both feel loved and supported by each other (feeling)

4. **Original Goal:** "I want to help my parents."
   Specific Goal: "I want my parents to be able to live with my family and cover their living costs before they turn 80."

   ▸ Own a four-bedroom home with a custom designed separate living space for my parents (metric)
   ▸ Support them financially with an extra $2,000 per month for living expenses (metric)
   ▸ Take them on quarterly trips to see their friends and relatives (activity)
   ▸ Feel they are secure and supported (feeling)

Keep in mind, you don't have to set a vision to be a superhero in each category, but you should have some type of standard for yourself. Focus on having integrity about what type of life you want to build. Ask yourself what is most important to you. For example, we have never felt the need to be Ironman champions or even run a half marathon. These are great goals, but they won't be in our future vision because we would prefer to invest differently into our health and have more moderate exercise goals.

Oftentimes, putting this Life Vision together can still feel overwhelming. Few people know exactly what they want their Life Vision to be 10 years from now, let alone 30. What helped us in putting a framework together is to ask the question in another way: What are some things you *don't want* 10 years from now? Putting a list together of what we don't want can be easier and help us define what we do want. This has been invaluable for us as we work on extending our vision two or three Life Phases into the future.

> **Craig here.** I knew in my soul I didn't want to have to work for someone else forever. I didn't care as much how I did this or by what means, but it was this burning desire that drove me to begin visualizing how I wanted to live at 35 when I was 25. Because this was a dominant thought process, I could also start to project certain things I wanted to create at 45. Now I'm not 45 yet, but it is remarkable how many of the things I did visualize with specificity have come true.

Step 5: Map Out Your 5- and 10-Year Life Vision

Figure 2.1 presents a sample 5- and 10-year Life Vision. Figure 2.2 is a Life Vision sheet for you to complete. In addition, you can find a downloadable PDF or spreadsheet on our website: tandemconsulting.co. Prioritize filling out this document as you complete this chapter. As you continue to progress through the book, we encourage you to reference this as a working document. By the time you finish reading this book, we want you to have your vision sheet fully completed and have the clarity we have been talking about.

FIGURE 2.1 **5- and 10-Year Life Vision**

Annual Mantra: "Learning and *applying* something new every day"

	VALUE #1	VALUE #2	VALUE #3	VALUE #4	VALUE #5
Family Member #1	Integrity	Challenge	Passion	Compassion	Spiritual
Family Member #2	N/A				
Side Hustle/Business	N/A				

CATEGORY	#	GOAL	TYPE	CURRENT STATE	5 YEAR STATE	10 YEAR STATE
Finances	1	Net Worth	Metric	-$15,000	$200,000	$500,000 (Half-Millionaire)
	2	Annual Income	Metric	$60,000	$90,000	$50,000 (20 hrs/week)
	3	Side Hustle Income	Metric	0	$30K/Year, ($10K Progress-Passive)	$100,000/Year ($50K Passive)
	4	Quarterly Budget Review	Activity	No	YES	YES
Health	1	Exercising Habits	Activity	Think About Running!	Run 3/week	Run 5/week
	2	Happy & Healthy	Feeling	Feel Unhealthy	Feel Healthy	Excellent Health & Example
	3	1 Mile Run Time	Metric	9 Minutes	7:30	6:30
	4	Mental	Activity	Meditate 1/Week	Meditate + Monthly Counseling	Meditate Daily
Spiritual	1	Religious Service	Activity	Attending Monthly	Attend Weekly	Attend Weekly
	2	Leadership Role	Activity	N/A	Join 2 Committees	Hold Exec Leadership Role
	3	Connection with God	Feeling	Distant/Low	Growing/Good	Intimate/Strong
	4	Charitable Donations	Metric	$1,000/Year	$5,000/Year	$10,000/Year
Relationships	1	Girlfriend Date Night	Activity	Weekly	Get Married! 2 Nights/Week	5 Nights/Week!!!
	2	Time with Children	Activity	N/A	N/A	2-3 Hours/Daily (Minimum)
	3	Create New Friendships	Metric	0!	2/Year	2/Year
	4	Feeling of Family Unity	Feeling	N/A	High Unity	High Unity
Recreation	1	Vacations Per Year	Activity	1–2 Weeks/Year	3 Full Weeks/Year	3 Months/Year
	2	Learn Guitar	Activity	N/A	Can Play Basic Chords	Can Play Basic Rock Songs
	3	Golf Handicap under 10	Metric	Handicap = 20	Handicap = 20	Handicap = 10
	4	General Happiness	Feeling	OK	Feel Joy & Fulfilled	Feel Joy & Fulfilled
Other/Misc.	1	Public Speaking	Activity	2 Events/Year	4 Events/Year	Monthly Speaking Event
	2	Home Improvement Proj	Activity	None	Redo Bathroom	Build New Garage
	3	Buy Lakehouse	Activity	N/A	N/A	Buy 2 Bedr Lakehouse

FIGURE 2.2 **5- and 10-Year Life Vision**

Annual Mantra:

	VALUE #1	VALUE #2	VALUE #3	VALUE #4	VALUE #5
Family Member #1					
Family Member #2					
Side Hustle/Business					

CATEGORY	#	GOAL	TYPE	CURRENT STATE	5 YEAR STATE	10 YEAR STATE
Finances	1					
	2					
	3					
	4					
Health	1					
	2					
	3					
	4					
Spiritual	1					
	2					
	3					
	4					
Relationships	1					
	2					
	3					
	4					
Recreation	1					
	2					
	3					
	4					
Other/Misc.	1					
	2					
	3					
	4					

Recommendations for Developing a Crystal-Clear Life Vision

1. Don't create a Life Vision based on what other people or society thinks it should be. Shredding others' or societal expectations of a meaningful life is critical in building a fulfilling and happy life. Oftentimes, parents' expectations are particularly influential in shaping a person's future. Investing time meditating on what you value and what is important is necessary.

2. Your vision is a *living, breathing* entity. Return to it quarterly or monthly, and revisit, refine, and add as necessary. Have fun with the process, and reference it frequently when discussing future dreams or goals.

3. Make the vision *visible*. Post it or elements of it in a place where all vested parties can see. Sign an agreement, create a mantra, or go straight-up dork patrol and make family hats or T-shirts (no visors please).

4. For those who have a significant other, work to put your 10-year vision together—*together*. Please do not put your goal of world domination in full motion and forget to include the Queen. Or the King. *Not* cool. When they are age appropriate, engage your children. They absolutely add to the jollification and creativity, and by helping them understand some of the family's long-term goals or mission, they can begin to appreciate and maybe even understand why you are working or why you can't play "Guess Who" with them *every* hour of the day. Putting together your Life Vision with your team, partners, or life mate should be enjoyable. Make an annual date night out of it!

Staying the Course with Your Life Vision

Along the journey you will need to execute some trade-offs for your success. *It needs to be purchased.* Some of these trades are easy, even upgrades, and some purchases are painfully difficult. It is during those challenging trade-offs that you have to be resolute on your vision's importance.

Of course, there are times when being truthful means you may need to change your vision. There is nothing wrong with making adjustments or a total changeup, as long as you are being *honest* with yourself about what you value.

Craig's goal by age 30 was to be a financially independent bachelor traveling the Mediterranean on a houseboat with a few best friends. Instead, he fell in love and got married at 29. The idea of living on a houseboat was still on the table for Carrie, but she was *adamant* about Craig letting go of his bachelor status. Goals and perspectives change—thus is life. Just make sure you are not giving up because the adventure has been more tumultuous than you planned. In our experience and observations, the journey to acquire something meaningful is almost *always harder* than you anticipate, no matter the endeavor.

> It continues to amaze us how many people are unwilling to truly *fight* hard for the life they want. What other battle is more paramount?

People often let the struggle or challenges along the path hamper their destination, feeling the journey is not worth the effort. We understand having fleeting hard feelings and real-life experiences of defeat. Setbacks are rarely fun. Occasionally you may need to allow yourself the freedom to feel bad. Maybe you need a weekend dipping potato chips directly into the ice cream tub, rewatching all nine Star Wars episodes. Go for it, but then freaking *dust yourself off* and get back on the field.

However, having some downtime, injured reserve, or off time is not a good justification to *quit* on your Life Vision. We are not talking about a pickup game of basketball or a 5K run for a sporting personal challenge—the subject at hand is *your life*.

We believe if the vision and goals are honest, clear, and holistic, it's less likely you will be in your final phase of life with major regrets. We can't get time back no matter how much we wish, and so much of *skilled living* comes from knowing what we value and aligning our actions and daily living with those values. If you know where you are going with purpose and clarity, it is easier to align your actions and daily decisions accordingly.

Just by doing the activities recommended in this chapter, your chance of creating your desired future state increases dramatically. We know, as we have lived and implemented this in our own family. We believe it will work for yours as well.

– – –

Now that we have done some work on your Life Vision, let's move on to one of the most influential aspect of our lives and in creating a successful side hustle—and it probably isn't what you would expect. Most turn immediately to the WHAT, meaning what their actual business is, but we instead implore you to start with the WHO.

CHAPTER 3

Finding Your WHO

It Takes a Village to Side Hustle

> *Show me an individual and I'll show you*
> *someone who had real positive influences in his*
> *or her life. I don't care what you do for a living—*
> *if you do it well, I'm sure there was someone*
> *cheering you on or showing the way. A mentor.*
> —Denzel Washington

What keeps most people from being successful business owners? Is it a lack of work ethic, ambition, intelligence, or capital? Some say success happens only if you "find your WHY" and develop a strategic plan of WHAT you should do next. In fact, that is the typical model: start with WHY, then move to WHAT. We disagree.

We believe it is one's mindset—how and what one thinks— that is a primary driver of one's ability to succeed. However, where do people acquire their mindset from? The answer: from the *WHO*, their environment, their associations. Therefore, we propose a paradigm shift: To move from your WHY to your WHO, *before* the WHAT or the HOW. To focus on the WHO earlier in the game. You can be an expert in your field, but if you don't have the right influences, it will be difficult to change from employee-based thinking and build your side hustle to a substantial level.

Imagine if you were born in the same physical body, the same genetics, but to a different family in another part of the world. There is a high chance your profession, education, religion, health, diet, social customs, and the language you speak would *all* be different. What does this tell you about the magnitude of this imprinting if you spoke a different language, had a different career, and perhaps had a completely different outlook on life? Human beings are designed to adapt; this is arguably why people take radically longer to become self-sufficient versus any other species. People are highly programmable, and their associations, family, teachers, coaches, mentors, and role models are driving that programming, how they think—and ultimately how they live. There is data suggesting that one's zip code, not one's genetics, is the biggest single determinant of one's success. We acknowledge that we were both given a strong start in terms of our own privilege, socioeconomic status, and access to education, to name a few, and that many individuals have a bigger mountain to climb among other barriers that have shaped their opportunities. This is one of many reasons why we feel that a strong WHO is of great importance and worth pursuing no matter your starting point.

Ironically, we see many side hustlers aspiring to move from the employee mindset to a successful business owner mindset, but *then never associate with people who are successful business owners*. This is like attempting to learn Mandarin but without associating with someone who speaks it. It's not that it can't be learned, but what's the probability you will become fluent? And on what timeline? Why would the world of business ownership be any different?

Once we become adults, being intentional about our associations is one aspect of life where we have control. We must be wise with WHO and WHAT you let influence your mind, decisions, and the quality of your thinking. This chapter addresses the importance of one's associations in relation to building a side hustle.

> **People are highly programmable, and their associations, family, teachers, coaches, mentors, and role models are driving that programming, how they think—and ultimately how they live.**

Popular books on business and entrepreneurship almost always have a section or chapter on mentorship and your associations, but too often as a side note, implying it's nice to have *if* you can get it. We don't view the WHO as a garnish or a side dish, but as the main course.

So why are so few people talking about this when we are all undeniably massive products of our environment? The current paradigm in business self-help is to begin with WHY, and yes, that is a good place to start, but when it comes to executing, it takes a village to start, build, and sustain a side hustle. We believe the current sequence for achieving one's Life Vision is ineffective. It looks like this:

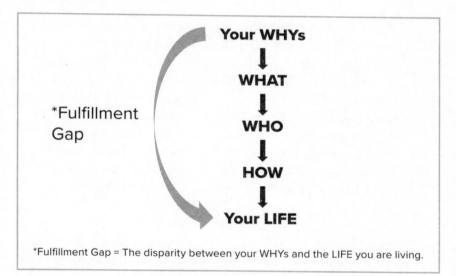

*Fulfillment Gap = The disparity between your WHYs and the LIFE you are living.

1. **The WHY.** The WHY is purpose driven. It's often vague, and many fumble to attach it to tangible goals or to sync it with a holistic Life Vision. But nonetheless at a young age we make a half-hearted attempt, and that weak attempt often becomes a driving force for the rest of our lives.

2. **The WHAT.** Pick your discipline, training, or area of study at 18 to 20 years old and base it on what interests you, what you are good at (or what you've been told you are), what will help you make relatively solid money, or what work you enjoy. Said discipline is rarely synergized with your WHY. This void

becomes the source of frustration and pain for so many, but is often unnamed, unidentified. It is the gap between your values, your talents, your desires, and what you spend your day doing. We call this the "Fulfillment Gap." This WHAT becomes one's livelihood, but often remains disconnected from one's deepest WHY.

3. **The WHO.** Once you arrive on the scene in your academic studies, apprenticeship, or career, someone is there waiting to train or teach you the skills necessary to be effective.

4. **The HOW.** The WHO now teaches you HOW to accomplish this line of work.

5. **Your Life (the Vision).** The vision now becomes a function of, or even hostage to, the WHAT. Your lifestyle and mindset are now being downloaded from the WHO in the environment that is submissive to the WHAT. Oftentimes, this thinking has already been preconditioned by your childhood and family. The programming gets reinforced even deeper as everything your family told you about making income and lifestyle are now being confirmed by your adult environment. You are following in your parents', bosses', and coworkers' footsteps. Supported by them. Advised by them. Influenced by them. Affirmed by them. *Your life is being shaped by them.*

We propose beginning with your Life Vision and letting that be your primary driver instead of using the traditional funnel described. The preceding process map, of course, works for many, but because one aspect of our Life Vision included stepping away from our corporate jobs at a young age, we knew we needed an alternative sequence; this sequence featured a different level of intention around the WHO and elevating this earlier on in the process. If your Life Vision is radically different from the people you grew up with, those who taught you in school, or those you currently associate with, then you need to make some radical changes with where you anchor the WHO on your timeline.

Let's flip the switch on the old paradigm to see what happens when we position the WHO as a more dominant priority. Here is an alternative process map that worked for us:

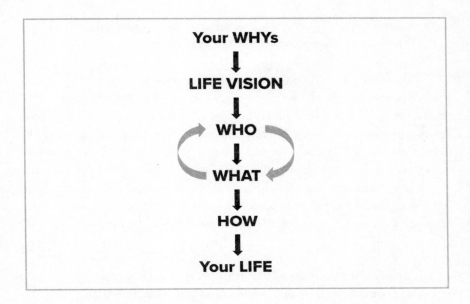

1. **The WHY(s).** How do you want to live? What type of person do you want to become? What are your core values? What is your purpose?
2. **The LIFE VISION.** What is the Life Vision you want to create? As stated in Chapter 2, this is a manifestation of your WHY(s), an overarching, holistic summary of what you value, the destination in your GPS. It also includes specific metrics, targets, and attributes that define your future.
3. **The WHO.** Find and identify someone who is living out, has lived, or is in the process of achieving your Life Vision. This should include both a mentor(s) and a supportive community. Instead of fumbling around trying to determine WHAT will take you there, start learning from those *WHO have already done it.*
4. **The WHAT.** Through the WHO you can often find the WHAT that will help you achieve and advance. But now you are learning from someone or an association that is copasetic and in alignment with your Life Vision.
5. **The HOW.** The WHO can help you with HOW to manifest this. They have already done it! This is extremely critical and simple logic many apply when it comes to sports, riding a bike, learning a foreign language, but then don't when it comes to life. The right

WHO can be there the whole way, assisting, modeling, and supporting you in accomplishing the Life Vision.

When Craig arrived on the corporate scene with a Fortune 50 company, he had several bosses who were great to work with and learn from. He also had a couple bosses whose bitterness and unhappiness were palpable. Not exactly the people he wanted to be modeling or impacting him, consciously or subconsciously. But none of his former bosses, coworkers, or managers had the lifestyle or the vision he had, so oftentimes their advice ran contrary to what he wanted to accomplish. This is concerning and an example of the common, unquestioned experience many have, and why so many people can never reach their full potential, let alone their deeper life goals.

> **A primary motivation of this book is to not only give you permission, but also encourage you to actively and intentionally pursue the people who are aligned with where you want to go, how you want to live, and what type of person you want to become.**

We recommend seeking out people well-established in their success. Identify people who have 2-to-100 times your spiritual, athletic, relationship, or financial well-being, as opposed to your peers. Even more important, search for people who have 2-to-100 times your level of happiness and wisdom.

> **Craig here.** I remember very clearly sitting in MBA school and listening to a professor share his thoughts on why the Porsche Cayenne wasn't going to be successful. He was an academic and well spoken, but while in class I missed a phone call from my mentor. And I thought: Why am I missing a phone call from the person who has the lifestyle that I want because I'm learning from a professor who seemingly does not? On the next break I got up, walked outside, called my mentor back, and never took another MBA class again.

Accessing the WHO *earlier* in your Life Phases and side hustle adventure lets you capture a real-life example of what you are aspiring to create and manifest in your Life Vision. It crystallizes so many things, including and most important, *not only that the vision is possible but also that the dream is real*, even if no one else you know, outside your discovered WHO, has ever created it.

Many people believe they already have a mentor through content consumption (reading good books or watching YouTube videos, etc.). However, a podcast can't customize recommendations for you. And when you are an entrepreneurial neophyte, it is especially difficult to know how to contextualize or when to apply the content. This is where a lot of people start patchworking advice and expertise together, which doesn't hold a candle to an actual mentor who knows you, and is invested in you, if not financially then relationally or emotionally.

So where and how do you find this magical WHO?

Mentorship

For us, mentorship has played such a deep role in achieving our Life Vision that it is difficult to articulate.

> **Our mentors have often opened doors for us we didn't even know existed.**

People often picture mentorship as a formal lunch or cup of coffee every 180 days with a corporate "mentor," and that's the extent of the relationship and their access to the other person's mindset. They give you some random advice, and you think "wow, that's so insightful." Then you try to implement it and randomly talk months later—assuming they are still willing to have coffee with you or you even both still work at the firm.

We view mentorship as something very different. There is something so deeply powerful about having a mentor that it is nonnegotiable in our minds. Not only can they help you navigate the terrain of your industry or start a business, but a great mentor can significantly improve the quality of your life. Best-selling author John Maxwell on his personal blog (johnmaxwell.com) defines mentorship as

> someone who teaches, guides, and lifts you up by virtue of his or her experience and insight. They're usually someone a little farther ahead of you on the path—though that doesn't always mean they're older! A mentor is someone with a head full of experience and heart full of generosity that brings those things together in your life.

These are individuals with whom you share very similar goals, values, and usually long-term relationships. A mentor can act as a lighthouse when the water gets rough; they can keep you on course and often illuminate the solution like no one else can.

We recommend identifying someone who has your desired future state (Life Vision), not just success in one particular subject matter. If someone has success in a specific technical expertise, that's great, but we consider that more of a coach. The best coaches, teachers, professors, and mentors are people who can help you off the court as much as on. Someone you can confide in personally as well as professionally. Why? Because often one's personal struggles prevent them from growing professionally versus the profession itself. Remember, side hustle work is not done in a silo.

Great Mentors

A great mentor will:

- ► Provide you with a real-life example of success. They help the vision seem more viable and possible. Being able to interact with them on a regular basis provides you the incremental boosts of belief you need on your journey.
- ► Customize their advice and recommendations for you.
- ► Call you on your bullsh**. Your subordinates or other people in the industry are less capable or likely to do this.
- ► Point out major roadblocks. They recognize trends, patterns, and possible signs of trouble oftentimes long before you see the challenge developing, as they have already walked the path.
- ► Empathize. Someone who has already completed the journey, or is much further ahead, understands your pain in ways that your closest friends and family may not. In the process of scaling a legitimate

business, they can provide both the support and solace that most cannot.

So why is it that so many people don't ever acquire a mentor? What holds people back? Here are a few reasons someone (namely, you) may not have acquired the type of mentor we are beginning to define:

- ▶ Your ego is too big. You unfortunately think you know it all. Why would you want anyone else's help? What value could they really add?
- ▶ You think entrepreneurship is about going at it alone and that you have to be a cowboy in the Wild, Wild West. The mindset is "If you didn't build it from scratch or you take too much help from others, you aren't a real or authentic entrepreneur."
- ▶ You are inexperienced and don't realize the extreme value a mentor and good association provides. You have undervalued it out of naivety.
- ▶ You don't know how to find one or are too scared or shy to ask someone. Just because a great mentor can be hard to find, doesn't mean you shouldn't pursue one!

> Our experience is many people do not pursue a mentor, because they think it is too difficult or they are not worthy of their potential mentor's time. This is a deeper-rooted challenge we address more in Chapter 6, but without the belief that you deserve this type of relationship, it is nearly impossible to acquire it! This doesn't mean you shouldn't be respectful of someone's time, but being respectful and being worthy are completely different.

Qualities of a First-Rate Mentor

1. **They demonstrate results.** They have accomplished, are close, or well on their way to where you want to be. They live how you want to live or are at least well on their way.
2. **They are willing to help and are accessible.** You can find the world's greatest mentor or someone at the top of their game, but

if you don't have genuine access, it is very difficult for them to get to know you and provide support. If they don't have time or are unwilling to make it, their influence is limited at best.

3. **Their values align with yours and they have pure intentions.** It is important to identify a mentor who has similar fundamental values. If you have a core value of investing time with your family, be mindful of identifying mentors who respect those priorities. You don't need to be an exact replica of your mentor, but an overarching alignment goes a long way.

4. **They have a vested interest.** Maybe they are at a point in their career or journey when they want to give back. Maybe they like you or see some of themselves in you and want the joy of paying it forward. Perhaps they want someone they can trust to take over their book of business or run their agency when they depart. Or potentially they can acquire some small ownership in a company you are building and be vested in the performance of the firm. Any of the preceding can work. Of course, the more vested they are, the easier it is to get their time and genuine support. Learning how to tie yourself to or create a symbiotic relationship with a mentor is not something commonly discussed—but we have found it invaluable. Get creative and offer them a micro percentage of your firm if they will be on your advisory board, or ownership at a deeply discounted rate, or a distribution if the firm acquires a certain level of profitability. How much money would you pay to have a Richard Branson, Bill Gates, Arianna Huffington, or a *Shark Tank* investor mentor you? Treat your real-life mentor similarly.

For the record, we are much bigger proponents of giving someone a stake or financial vested interest in the long-term performance of your business versus an upfront consulting fee or an early payout. This ties them to the long-term *performance* of you and your business. People tend to act and behave based on how they are rewarded, mentors included.

How to Find a Quality Mentor?

Top-notch mentors are not always easy to find, nor should they be. The more they have accomplished, the harder it is to access them, their thinking, and their time. Different avenues are available to finding mentors including:

- ▸ Networking through family, friends, and associates
- ▸ Engaging with or direct messaging on social media
- ▸ Formal networking events
- ▸ Owners of companies
- ▸ Referrals
- ▸ Industry periodicals
- ▸ Phone calls
- ▸ Emails, text, WhatsApp, or WeChat messaging
- ▸ Lunches, coffees, chai, golf, beer, tequila shots

When you find someone you believe would make a terrific mentor, here are some steps to begin building a relationship and *earn* their mentorship. Realize they are already successful and busy and have other people vying for their time. You must be confident in your approach, which means you've considered thoroughly why you chose this person as a possible mentor. Have something to offer back, and work to connect around values, intention, and even chemistry. You want to stand out, let them know your earnestness in learning from them, create a win as to why they should invest time into you, and be steadfast in your follow-up. A few additional tips:

- ▸ Find a referral or warm introduction if possible.
- ▸ When you approach them, be transparent about your intentions.
- ▸ Do your research! Don't ask them questions like "What was your first company?" or "Where did you go to school?" when it may be easily posted on their LinkedIn profile or company website.
- ▸ Demonstrate your seriousness, accountability, teachability, and a willingness to learn! This might take some time.
- ▸ Offer to give something back in return such as time on a project, expertise for one of their businesses, a nod on social media, or help with a nonprofit they support.
- ▸ Be persistent! If they initially seem resistant, continue to *respectfully enroll* or serve them with the quality of your work, your intentions, and your consistency. We have mentored many people over the years as a function of their building a consistent case for mentorship.

You don't have to shoot for someone outrageously successful or a billionaire to be your mentor. If you are looking to get into investing, you might not need to *start* with Warren Buffett. Most professional athletes were learning beyond the basics from a little league or high school coach before the Phil Jacksons of their industry began "mentoring" them.

Although some mentors might need some financial incentive, many great mentorship relationships do not require this. By joining a dues-driven group such as Toastmasters, the National Speakers Association, or another industry association, one can often access people who want to provide support. It is human nature to want to help, but it's critical you pursue the environment and take the initiative to ask.

How to Maximize Time with Your Mentor

As mentioned, if mentors are worth their salt, they are busy, and you have limited access to their time. So how you use that time matters.

- ▶ Be prepared. When you have an opportunity to connect, come absolutely prepared and ready to impress with the quality of your questions and quality of your listening. Ask thoughtful questions and be comfortable asking follow-up questions when you don't understand something. A few examples: "I understand what you are advising, but from my experience that doesn't seem like a good idea because of X and Y. Can you help me better understand your mindset behind this recommendation?" "What are some of the most common mistakes you see people in my situation make, and how would you recommend avoiding them?" "What do you think might be my biggest blind spot or weakness? How would you recommend I grow in this area?"
- ▶ Seek to understand the *why behind their thought process* versus just the surface-level activity, number, or strategy they may recommend. Many mentees botch this. If you don't understand the deeper thinking, you fail to apply the principal or mindset in an alternative context. Go deeper.
- ▶ Be mindful and respectful of their time, but do not be timid about asking for that time! You likely have to follow up, take initiative, and oftentimes fight to keep the relationship.
- ▶ Be sure to implement what they advise and talk to them about your implementation. Little is more frustrating for a mentor than to provide advice they know is helpful, but then never see it applied by the

mentee, especially when the mentee keeps requesting more time and support. Once you've applied the advice, be sure to communicate how it helped or what the results were in the next conversation.

▶ Make sure you are getting honest feedback from your mentor. Ask, beg, plead, or if necessary, pay them to give you high-caliber feedback. Positive *and* negative—their perspective is unique to most others in your life who are operating as counterparts, employees, or family and friends.

▶ Thank them, formally. Maybe it's a thoughtful card, email, small gift, event, or connection you can create, preferably memorable or unique.

▶ Build and retain an authentic relationship over time that can become truly personal. Get to know what's important to them.

▶ Always keep them in your circle! Just because a mentor has helped you achieve in a certain arena doesn't mean they can't continue to bring value, even if you have left that arena. Sometimes you may have even surpassed them in certain ways, but the reality is they still carry unique experiences, perspectives, and wisdom that you do not!

Carrie here. After a conversation with a mentor, my goal is to be able to answer "why?" to the recommendations that were given to me so it's not just regurgitated information. I want to have actually leveled up and strengthened my ability to think. And as important as it is to ask thoughtful questions, don't have a million. It's just as valuable to get an expert going on a tangent or a riff. Often, you get the most candid, unedited, and valuable mindset when you create a space for someone successful to free flow. It's usually a powerful open-ended question followed by good listening that takes the conversation to this next level of extraction.

Having more than one mentor can be a great benefit. Different mentors can guide you and support you in different ways and bring unique strengths to the table. However, we have also seen side hustlers chase down new mentors too frequently or have too many at one time. Having 10 or 11 mentors simultaneously, in the way we are defining it, will likely cause confusion and create conflict, as each has their own perspective. Identify a couple key mentors in your life and stay with them. Unless you lose confidence in their character or genuine capacity to empower you, stay steady. There is value in continuity, especially when you have cleared the honeymoon phase of a mentor/mentee relationship—when it's no longer new, but real.

Also, moving forward in life is often a function of our discipline to dial into the people who can pull us forward. Even if you get access to them for only a small percentage of your time, you have to intentionally elevate and weight this time accordingly. And although you may get access to your *mentor* for small pockets of time, the *community* you surround yourself with can build on this concentrated thought process and also create a more regular and accessible support system.

Building Your Community

An ideal business community is a crew of people who are in similar industries and have an overlapping vision and mindset that support *and* also challenge you. Some of these individuals might even be your competitors, which creates a positive environment for leveling up. Your community can be extremely diverse, but also have a common thread or trajectory that pulls the group together toward a joined goal or mission. A shared mission or theme helps develop a culture, an environment, that is extremely powerful in creating the pull for you to keep growing, holding you accountable in ways you can't duplicate going solo, and taking away excuses that the rest of the world would validate. This community also provides invaluable camaraderie that keeps morale high despite the natural ups and downs that come with being a side hustler. Without this group you are a lone wolf in harsh conditions.

Everyone should prioritize finding their pack. Finding a community of people who "get you" in ways that people who have known you for decades don't or can't is crucial in your success. In Chapter 9 we discuss how to build an inner circle more intricately involved in your business—meaning the people you hire to consult, service, or work alongside you as you brand and raise capital for your side hustle. Here we are focused more on the emotional and psychological power of finding like-minded people, with experienced and informed backgrounds that give you tools and anecdotal wisdom to help you stay the course.

So how do you find these people? What does building a community and support group look like? Here are a few specific tips that have worked for us:

▸ Seek associations within your niche industry.
▸ Identify associations that have a winning culture and are forward moving; there is *momentum* and people are growing.
▸ Look for other individuals with strong leadership.
▸ Inquire about other associations or individuals recommended by your mentor. Sometimes other mentees who have worked with your mentor can be a top-shelf resource!
▸ Find associations and individuals you feel you can genuinely learn from and return value to.
▸ Build additional relationships outside of your industry. These are commonly called mastermind or referral groups and are not only practical from a morale-building standpoint, but also can be great sources of referral business.

While you might find many of your best connections within your industry, it's also important to develop some diversity within your posse. This might not be your primary inner circle, but peripheral people within your sphere of influence whom you support, and vice versa. For example, they might be professionals, entrepreneurs, and side hustlers in your local area whom you get to know at regular networking events or with whom you have a lot of mutual connections. In addition, here are a few other places you can look to build supportive relationships that may fall outside your industry:

▸ BNI (Business Network International) groups
▸ Churches, mosques, temples, and so on
▸ Athletic or fitness groups
▸ Other interest groups (dogs, bird-watchers, *Star Trek* fans, etc.)
▸ Businesses

- Rotary, Kiwanis, or other service organizations
- Volunteer groups and nonprofits
- Facebook or Meetup groups
- LinkedIn or in-person local LinkedIn events
- Mastermind groups
- Build your own association! (this could be using any of the above examples).

Carrie here. In my experience it's so important to have an investment mindset in any type of association you want to gain access to. It's easy to have a mentality where you show up late, bounce early, and leave all the responsibility to other members of the group. However, as with anything, what you put in is what you get out. This works the same for relationships. If you approach these spaces with a giving mindset versus taking, you ultimately receive tenfold as a function of your contribution over time. As a result, there's deeper integration, support, and synergy that gets built, which are some of the biggest benefits of tapping into an association to begin with.

Ensure Your Community Challenges and Elevates You

Associating with your peers can provide crucial support to lean on; however, just as we advise with finding mentors, try to include people who challenge and elevate your game in your community. How do you do that?

First, embrace and study your competitors' thought process, mindset, work habits, strategies, processes, and products. Continually challenge yourself to access those playing at a higher level. If you're not stretched by your association to where you are uncomfortable, identify people who can. It's an amazing ego trip to be the most successful person in the room, but if you are interested in growth, that's not always the best play.

In addition, don't be afraid to upgrade your community over time if stagnation sets in. Of course, being loyal to the people and relationships you develop along the way is important. But there comes a time when you may evolve beyond a certain sphere of influence, or you remain, but in more of a leadership/consulting capacity. This is oftentimes a natural evolution and an important realization that entrepreneurs sometimes miss.

Craig here. For about 10 years of my life I dabbled with meditating. I would meditate sporadically for a few weeks or month only for it to fade to the background of my busy life. Last year, I finally took my own advice and identified a clear WHO, a group of dedicated local practitioners, people who have been practicing for decades at one to two hours a day and regularly complete extended meditation retreats. I immediately felt a sense of communion, pull, and accountability, and this association has radically improved my consistency. Although I have a long way to go in my practice, *I am consistently practicing*, a function of this association. Through this association I started engaging with people probably a thousand times further along in their meditation practice and have found a wonderful mentor as well.

I've made more progress with my meditation in 1 year of engaging with a community and a having a mentor than in 10 years of going it alone. Without the accountability, cheerleading, moral support, and guidance of like-minded people, I probably would have continued my frustrating start-stop performance for decades to come. In my experience, side hustling is no different.

Disassociating

Disassociating, creating separation of mindset, time spent with certain people and overall influence is an important part of life. In our experience this type of pruning, is about mindfulness. As you form your associations, build your community, and seek out valuable mentors, disassociating can be a sensitive topic. As such, we challenge you to take a half step back and begin to evaluate how and who you invest your time with. Your time is both valuable and finite, and who you choose to spend or invest it with makes an impact on your ability to achieve your Life Vision.

It continues to amaze us how many people give away their most precious resource based on a feeling of general social obligation or blind conditioned programming. It's OK to say a graceful no when you need to. And if you feel a real internal conflict, consider creative ways you can make it up if an important event needs to be missed or cut short. A lot of times with loved ones or extended relatives, investing quality one-on-one time can go further than just showing up to a big event that doesn't really enrich your relationship with them.

We should all take stock and do some pruning—or weeding! You can't risk being distracted by people who aren't helping you on some level get closer to your vision—even if it's that they are generally an energy suck. To identify whom you might need to disassociate from, we recommend dividing your associations into the following groups: toxic, negative, neutral, or actively supportive. Note, disassociating does not mean no longer talking to family members or breaking up with friends from high school. It means knowing who to include in the inner workings of your plans for your side hustle and your Life Vision. Here are some ways to manage the different types of people in your life:

Toxic: These people have strong negative energy and add very difficult interpersonal dynamics to their environment. Their toxicity affects others. Minimize your exposure and their influence. If this happens to be a boss or close coworker, consider changing your job or your role. If it happens to be a close family member, set boundaries for your own mental health. Therapy can be a great outlet for learning how to navigate these types of relationships! A mentor or general positive association can help dilute toxic influences in your life, however you'll still need to do the hard work of developing a healthy dynamic with these types of people.

Negative: These are the naysayers, the ones pointing out the flaws in your plan (not in a helpful way), touting stories of other's failed ventures, and are waiting for you to fail so they can be justified in their negative projections. These types of relationships can hold a lot of power and be much more common than toxic ones. Because their negativity is likely more subtle, the effect can linger. Of course, if you find yourself in these spheres of influence regularly, check to make sure *you* are not the source of negativity! Assuming you're not, here are a few recommendations to facilitate living a productive life while navigating other negative people.

- Limit your exposure. This strategy can vary greatly depending on the type of relationship you have with this person. If they are a random high school acquaintance or old coworker, it may be easier to do than with a close family member.
- Suit up your armor. Make the decision that their negativity can and will roll off your back. Take a deep breath and examine the source. We once had a friend who was negative about one of our business ventures. Since he was one of the worst money managers and decision makers we knew, it was actually a confirmation we were doing things right.
- Assess. Is there some truth to what they are sharing? If so, why is their negativity or commentary flustering you? Is the tone of their delivery potentially overshadowing the value in what they are saying? Is there an unresolved issue that you have not internally addressed—with your own belief in your side hustle or in your personal relationship with them? Take some time to think this through so their future commentary doesn't affect you as much emotionally.
- Tell them how you feel. Consider having an upfront conversation with them about how their actions have impacted you and what you are working to create. *Crucial Conversations: Tools for Talking When Stakes Are High* by Alan Switzler, Joseph Grenny, and Ron McMillan is an excellent book for preparing for some of these conversations.
- Revisit your own values and reconfirm why you are side hustling. You cannot control other people, but if you have a clear purpose with your activity, feel confident in what you are doing, and execute as much as possible on the preceding recommendations, then other people's negativity can be left for them to deal with.

Neutral: If something or someone isn't pulling you forward, ask yourself this: Are they slowing you down? In many ways, neutral associations can be the most dangerous. Many family members or longtime friends may fall into this category.

> **Realize, those who love us are not always qualified to empower us.**

- For example, suppose you are building a side hustle and working on a large contract to handle a client's social media account, and your good friends call and are going to the big game. They have good intentions, but they don't understand your current workload, and just want to have a good time. Trust your gut here and proceed how you wish. For us, our family and close inner circle get a special pass. We do not let many people in the neutral bucket sway us out of staying on point in the direction of our Life Vision. You may choose to go to the game, concert, or Dungeons and Dragons group role-play or not—just make sure your decision aligns with your values.
- Don't continue on the journey for their approval. Remember you are being driven by your own WHY, your own internal compass. We can assure you we did not write a book for the approval or recognition from our family or friends. Of course, it's great when they are supportive, but we don't adjust our life path for that type of support.
- If these are close friends and family, make sure to invest the quality time with them that feels honest. Our grandparents and parents will not be with us forever. For us building our side hustle and creating financial independence was extremely important so we could invest more time in these relationships. However, be careful that in that journey you don't blow important opportunities to invest time in the people you love the most—this is likely a key component of your Life Vision also!

Actively supportive: These are the people you are seeking and need to be intentional about pursuing their thinking and time to truly *grow* your business! This is the friend who offers to babysit because you have a presentation to write. This is the cousin who is your best customer and is outright cheering you on in your journey despite having a completely different path of her own. This is the former coworker who has their own side hustle, and you are mutually supporting one another's pursuits through book swaps and referrals.

Keep in mind few people can build and run successful businesses and cater to every extended family member, high school friend, fishing buddy, and past coworker at the same time. You have to choose what you value, and you vote with your time. You vote with your hours. Every hour spent is a vote cast, so vote intentionally.

— — —

Now that we have discussed your Life Vision and wrangling in your WHO, let's begin evaluating WHAT type of business you should be building. What is the best side hustle vehicle to carry you to that destination? Although luxury sports cars can be excellent vehicles, if your destination is Bali, you may want to consider other options.

CHAPTER 4

The WHAT

Choosing the Right Side Hustle for You

There's no shortage of remarkable ideas,
what's missing is the will to execute them.
Seth Godin

Most people are never trained to evaluate a business opportunity. In fact, they tend to stumble onto an idea based on a random association, industry, or skill they may already have. Or they may spend hours searching the internet only to feel overwhelmed and frustrated and not take *any action*. We often talk about ROI, return on investment, but keep in mind there's also COI, cost of inaction, which is the common story for many eternally aspiring entrepreneurs. Conversely, some are overeager, dropping hundreds or even thousands of dollars into online courses, coaches, or training that doesn't end up proving fruitful. There is nothing wrong with exploring or investing, but you don't want to be spinning your wheels for years. We want to equip you with the proper mindset and tools to effectively evaluate which side hustle is right for you so you capture the ROI you're looking for.

So WHAT type of business should you build? Remember that, based on the last chapter, identifying a strong WHO, a mentor who has already manifested a Life Vision similar to yours, can also help you identify, evaluate, and even build your WHAT. When determining your WHAT, think viability, not just what is the most easily accessible. It is natural for side hustlers to lean into their current domain or work experience to form a side hustle (a book editor becomes a free-lance writer; a real estate agent opens an Airbnb management arm). There is no doubt, if you already have experience or expertise in an industry, you may have an edge, but evaluating if your comfort zone and current skills set you up with the right medium to achieve your bigger Life Vision is key.

This chapter is designed to provide a framework and process to evaluate making quality decisions when deciding which side hustle is right for you. **Most people have been conditioned to be consumers and employees, but have never been trained on how to evaluate business opportunities or systems.**

And with your Life Vision being your primary driver and destination, we recommend being extremely flexible, assuming you're looking to reach your desired future state, not just doing what sounds the most exciting or familiar.

> **By being open minded and seeking opportunities that are most likely to be *successful*, you can increase the probability of achieving your goals.**

We want to help you evaluate your WHAT options, at both the micro and macro levels, whether you are scaling an already in-motion side hustle or still deciding which kind of business you'd like to start.

Step 1: What's Your Pre-Side Hustle Status?

For those still in the preplanning stage of your side hustle adventure, you need to consider your current situation to evaluate your readiness in building a side hustle. Ultimately, it's a leader's role to define reality. Meaning, you have to understand your reality and the genuine opportunities and challenges you face in relation to a side hustle. Here are some questions to help you assess your status.

1. **How much capital capacity do you have?** We have met many a millennial who wants to go heavy into real estate, build an app, create a professional disc golf league, or build an indoor soccer facility, but if you don't have the money or the willingness to borrow money, why burn the energy on something that isn't viable? In our mid-twenties, buying a traditional franchise restaurant was a good idea in theory, but in actuality, it was not a reasonable option. We didn't have the money it would take to launch a Taco Bell let alone the additional funds to scale and buy *more* franchises. It is also important to consider what businesses may align or clash with your values you identified back in the Life Vision chapter. As an example, although the fast-food industry can be profitable, there are many fast-food restaurants we would not want to be regularly promoting. So many businesses may get crossed off your list for these reasons.

    Ask yourself: *Do I have the capital, or am I willing to borrow the capital, to make this particular opportunity truly work for me? Is the risk required to create success acceptable?*

2. **Do you have the time capacity?** What amount of time are you willing to allocate toward building a business? When we were each single in our twenties, other than our jobs and family, time was relatively limitless. Now with several businesses and two small children, we have a different filter for evaluating new ventures. What are some current commitments you are unwilling to let go of? What are some you could tone down or drop if you were ready to commit to building a side hustle seriously? If you plan to keep your 40-plus-hour-a-week job, how can you factor in the time and energy to work your business?

    Ask yourself: *Can I effectively engage in this opportunity with the time resources I am willing to make available?*

3. **Do you have marketable expertise?** If you are a consultant with a major engineering firm, could you easily do some freelance consulting on the evenings and weekends? Do you already have an

expertise and trusted relationships with potential clients? Or if you have been working for a property management company, could you split off on your own and in your spare hours provide a similar service to property owners for a better price? Is this skill transferable to another industry or business opportunity?

Ask yourself: *Do I have a strong experience or deep expertise in a particular subject or market? Does it provide me with an edge in a particular industry—consulting, educational, or other type of business?*

4. **What is your entrepreneurial experience?** Have you done anything entrepreneurial in the past? Have you ever started a business before? What part of that process did you enjoy or not enjoy? Does product development, building a team from scratch, learning new skills, or bookkeeping excite you, or do you loathe some of these activities? If so, what are you willing to do until you can outsource, and what will you need a partner or consulting firm to handle?

Ask yourself: *Am I willing to learn the necessary skills to create success in this environment or with this opportunity? Or can I partner with someone who is?*

5. **Going back to the WHO, do you have entrepreneurial access?** Do you know any successful entrepreneurs who may be willing to mentor or support you? Have they created the success you would like, are they willing to truly help you, or can they refer you to someone who is?

Ask yourself: *Is there a solid WHO I can learn from that has used this vehicle, system, or business model and already created the lifestyle I desire? Can I access them or others who are further along on the journey and are they willing to genuinely help me?*

6. **How high is your risk tolerance?** How much risk are you comfortable with? Monetarily, legally, reputationally? You may not have hard answers to these questions, but it will be important to reference these when evaluating different opportunities.

Ask yourself: *How much risk will this opportunity require financially, reputationally, and legally? Are these risks identifiable and am I able to properly assess them?*

7. **Do you have the bandwidth to travel?** In our twenties travel was our hot button. Craig here. I remember telling my boss to send me

as far away and as often as possible. Now, we still love travel, but with a nice home, a lake house, kids, and most of our family local, flying to Los Angeles for 24 hours requires a different cost-benefit analysis.

Ask yourself: *Does this side hustle require you to travel? Is travel exciting, or do you dread airplanes, hotels, and long road trips? Can this business be built remotely?*

8. **Do you have the desire and skills to succeed in sales and marketing?** Many businesses that do not require a large amount of capital upfront often require a fair amount (if not a lot) of selling and/or marketing.

Ask yourself: *Will sales and marketing be a predominant role of this side hustle? Am I good at sales or is this an unknown? How can I find out and/or incrementally begin to grow these skills?*

9. **How critical is passion?** Many aspiring side hustlers mistakenly believe their business must be something they are passionate about. Although you certainly can be, you don't need to be. Like a job, for us the goal was to use a side hustle as a tool to bring us closer toward our Life Vision, whereby feeding our long-term passions.

Ask yourself: *Is this a side hustle I can see myself enjoying or being passionate about?*

Does My Business Need to Be My Passion?

The short answer: No.

It *can* be, but it absolutely does not *have* to be. Many people give the advice that if you want to start a business, you need to be passionate about it. We are not against this—but we want you to fully understand your options. A massive mistake we see people make is feeling like they *must* start a business around snowboarding, photography, or soccer because they love it.

When Carrie graduated school, her dream was to travel the world and capture the beauty of those travels via photos . . . in exchange for currency. After analysis on what that would take and what training it would require, she debated attending the Chicago Art Institute. After considering the six-plus figures of school debt on top of already having a four-year degree, and paying for a studio and other operating costs such as high-tech equipment, she put a pause on the plan to really assess the lifestyle it would create. Would any version of this plan be conducive to her overall Life Vision?

Her passion and love for taking photos did not necessarily align with the day-to-day uphill financial climb of needing to take photos for money to put food on the table. She felt much of the joy would be lost in the bustle to monetize. She loved the art and creativity too much. Not to say she couldn't have made this plan work, but opening her eyes to what life would look like versus the glorified version she daydreamed about was clarifying.

Answering the preceding questions is critical to knowing how to select the right type of business to build. You need your answers to complete our evaluation tool at the end of this chapter.

The WHAT: A Macro Discussion

When people think of what business they want to build, they often go specifically into the type of service or product. But first, we want you to have a broader macro knowledge of business on a categorical basis. These categories and the corresponding matrix at the end of this chapter will improve your capacity and ability to decipher what kind of business aligns with your Life Vision.

Before You Go For It: Evaluate Your Long-Term Goals

When aligning your side hustle with your Life Vision, it's important to understand exactly what role your side hustle needs to play. Determining the amount of income is important, but now that you have more context, we also need to understand the nature of that income when deciding what type of business to launch and how you will build that business. Here is a list of questions that can build a bridge between your business goals and your Life Vision.

1. What amount of money do I want my side hustle to generate?
2. What time frame do I want to accomplish this in?
3. How much ongoing time do I want, or am I willing to invest in, my side hustle?
4. How much money am I willing to invest?
5. How much risk can I take in this venture?
6. How much ongoing fulfillment do I need to receive from growing my side hustle? Meaning, how important is it to like, love, or be passionate about the work?
7. Do I have an interest in eventually selling the business and cashing out?

These may seem like overly simple questions, but many people have started a side hustle without a clear plan to scale or a true Live Vision they are working toward. They are literally just thinking, *Let me get a few more clients so I can make some more money.* It's important to go deeper and be more specific so we can avoid the Fulfillment Gap that often comes with traditional employment.

Active, Passive, and Progressive-Passive Incomes

On his website, Dave Ramsey writes:

> Passive income is money you earn in a way that requires little to no daily effort to maintain. Some passive income ideas— like renting out property or building a blog—may take some work to get up and running, but they could eventually earn you money while you sleep.

While many business owners can create passive income from their business, the majority do not. Robert Kiyosaki identifies this distinction as being self-employed (active income) versus owning a big business (passive income). His book *The Cash Flow Quadrant* is a great resource for better understanding the difference between these two types of businesses. In short, active income means you do all the work to keep the revenue flowing and passive means you don't!

Although it can be difficult to achieve fully passive income, there are ways to move a business or income stream in that direction, toward what we call *progressive-passive income*. Progressive-passive income occurs when the business owner expends effort, but the effort is still limited, minimal, or needed only periodically. For example, you could run a small car detailing business with a handful of contractors so that when you go on vacation your business still generates revenue.

Understanding the difference between these three types of business incomes is crucial in understanding how your side hustle can impact your lifestyle. Let's walk through a scenario to demonstrate our point: Two individuals have the ambition of leaving their full-time teaching jobs so they can stay home with their young children. They both buy similar small Airbnb rental properties.

▶ Person A wants to draw as much profit as possible, so they do all the internet marketing, guest communications, housekeeping, and maintenance on the property. They make decent money but not enough to replace their job income and consistently commit 10 to 15 hours of work per week to maintain the extra income. Their only mindset around scaling is the belief that it will require *another 15 hours of work* and more risk.

▶ Person B decides to outsource most of the rental activities to a property management company, making significantly less profit their first year, but enabling them to use their time to research more rentals. They end up buying two more properties that are more profitable, now that they know the game. After a couple years Person B generates *twice the profit and has minimal tasks they need to perform on a weekly basis.* They are also in a stronger position to continue to scale their operation should they choose. They step away from their job as they have fully replaced the income, and ultimately, they have *more time* to be with their children.

Person A now has less total income than Person B. They also have *less time* because they cannot leave their teaching job *and* they still have to manage the rental property. Person A has a side hustle with active income. Person B has a side hustle with passive income. The lifestyle differences are dramatic.

To the untrained eye and from the outside perspective, both individuals own rental property, but when you get under the hood and kick the tires, you may notice one is running ragged while the other is building wealth and creating a lifestyle with customization. Be mindful when you start a side hustle about what *type* of income you can make.

Here are a number of examples to illustrate the difference between building systems that can generate passive income versus work that typically does not:

ACTIVE INCOME	PROGRESSIVE- PASSIVE/PASSIVE INCOME
Real estate agent	Owning the agency
Restaurant owner	Owning 10 Subway franchises
Consultant	Build a consulting firm
Flip houses	Owning 20 multifamily rental units
Have one Airbnb	Have 30 Airbnbs and a property manager
Drive Uber	Own Uber!
Piano lessons	Create a piano MasterClass with video content
Sell Rodan & Fields	Develop a network of 100s of Rodan & Fields reps
Make and sell salsa	Own a salsa manufacturing company
Freelance writing	Write a book about freelancing and/or own an agency of freelance writers
Day trade	Oversee a team that manages a $100 million dollar portfolio
Electrician	Have 10 electricians working for you
Sell on eBay	Develop a course that teaches people to power sell on eBay

It is important to understand the lifestyle contrast between the left and right sides of this list. For the options that are solely self-employment based, they typically carry less risk and one has more control, but you're also always trading time for money. It is difficult to get real leverage on your efforts if you are a one-person show.

We had a skilled painter do work on our home recently, and he was actually turning many jobs *down* as he was getting so many requests for his labor. We asked why he wasn't hiring other painters to work for him, and he replied: "Managing people is too difficult, and they often do low-quality work." He was choosing the route of self-employment. However, if he had been willing to hire a team of five or six quality painters, personally train them, and hire a shift manager, then the amount of leverage on his time and income could increase substantially. Remaining self-employed is not necessarily bad, if he and his family are satisfied with the lifestyle that comes with it. Being self-employed does come with more control and initially less headaches than hiring and training others—but at what opportunity cost?

> The challenge for most people is they've never had an example, an association, or a mentor to help them both visualize and execute on how to upscale effectively.

Interestingly, when we asked the painter how he got into his line of work, he said he learned the business from his father—who was also self-employed.

Innovation or an Established System?

Many aspiring business owners make the mistake of thinking they need to create a completely original idea to build a successful side hustle. This is simply not true. *You don't have be an inventor to be a business owner.* We hear very little noise regarding this concept, and from a practical application, this may be one of the most important sections of this book.

When you think of the word *entrepreneur*, what comes to mind? Many think of a hardcore entrepreneur who develops an entirely new product in their mother's basement and uses it to change the world. They think of the Harvard or MIT college dropout whose destiny was to become a zillionaire—or the eccentric, the ultrarich, or the uberintelligent. This is *not* the *majority* of business owners.

When Craig was in commercial banking, he saw many business owners who have started out as side hustlers, make great incomes, and create magnificent lifestyles in relatively dull and boring industries, often using cookie-cutter systems they purchased, copied, inherited, or just improved.

Craig had former clients who made $1 million net a year selling pickles, lawnmowers, wood pallets, nuts and bolts, electrical boards, plumbing, or whatever. Several of these were started as side hustles. A former client, also probably worth $15 million in his late thirties, shared with Craig that he *netted $80,000* the prior year from a modest-sized trailer park. At the time Craig's banking salary was $86,000.

Many successful business owners haven't invented much of *anything*. They didn't necessarily have a genius idea or even an original idea; however, they might be individual franchisee owners of a McDonald's, Valvoline Oil Change, Jimmy John's, Anytime Fitness, or a RE/MAX real estate agency.

There are also many other examples of business systems, outside of franchising, that don't require you to develop an original product or an original system. A few examples include agencies, direct sales, rental property, affiliate marketing, drop shipping, and so on. There are also many platforms that allow you to grow your business or product, such as eBay, Amazon, VRBO, Instagram, Skillshare, Etsy, and YouTube.

Now, you may not have the $1 million it costs to buy a traditional franchise, but consider developing a MasterClass or leveraging Udemy, which have proven systems. There are also several lower-cost franchises you can launch for less, between $5,000 and $175,000, such as a commercial cleaning business, youth athletic or dance programs, or a leadership training program such as Dale Carnegie Training. Not only can proven models or *systems* produce great revenues and successful companies, they often come with the additional formulas, guidance, education, association, and vendor relationships that drastically improve your probability of success. That's the WHO, the WHAT, and the HOW in one shot.

> In addition, an established *business system* often comes with the ability to eventually *lean back into* the *proven formula*, creating a higher level of automation or passive income, giving you a greater chance to manifest a stellar lifestyle and your Life Vision.

In our early twenties we had minimal amounts of capital, credibility, experience, and skill, so it was a better play for us to leverage systems for our first businesses. There is nothing wrong with starting a business this way. It's these businesses that afforded us the experience, income, credibility, skills, *confidence*, and *time* to add on other projects, step away from our corporate lives, and chase our passion projects like public speaking, coaching, our children, and our nonprofit. **Do consider though: your *first* business doesn't need to be your *last* business.** In fact, if you are successful in the game of entrepreneurship, your first is unlikely to be your last or only business. It's rare for us to meet a successful entrepreneur who doesn't have that next opportunity or project in the queue.

Now, if you already have your business rolling or you want to pursue building something additional, original, or novel, *you still have to create a system if you want to scale it.* You have to source and build the product from scratch, make it functional, develop a demand in the marketplace for it, then generate a system to scale to a level that provides real value for you and your family. And there is always the risk that a major player can come along and duplicate your prototype and sell it for a fraction of the price due to their economies of scale.

Drawbacks of Using an Established System
Established systems often come with additional fees or costs and limited autonomy or creativity.

1. When leveraging already established systems, you have less creativity, which many people crave. Initially this can be a blessing, *as the lack of creativity often keeps you from running bad plays or making major follies.* However, once you have established some success and credibility, a franchise or other prebuilt system may feel restrictive. If you do your own thing, you won't have to ever check back with "Corporate" to confirm if a new product or marketing campaign needs to be approved. You maintain more agency and freedom to innovate. Also, when using established systems, you don't receive credit for creating the system, as you didn't make the product or create the idea; someone else did! For some entrepreneurs that sense of autonomy and feeling like they built something of their own carries a lot of value.

2. Most established systems come with some form of a franchising fee or other associated costs. Building something of your own does not carry this form of taxation. Keep in mind, you are essentially paying for a proven formula for success, refined processes, perhaps additional marketing, and so on. Franchise owners we have known often share to be mindful if the annual franchise fees are based off

of top-line revenue or net profit. Net profit is preferred, obviously. It can be painful to pay out a franchise or other overhead fees if you are not actually profitable.

Now that we have discussed some perspectives to consider when evaluating a business, you can start applying this mindset into real-world situations and begin appraising which opportunity is the best for you.

Evaluating Your Side Hustle Options

Figure 4.1 incorporates the many questions, concepts, pros and cons we have discussed around different business options, and allows you to compare and contrast different business opportunities in a holistic way.

Please note: This evaluation chart is meant exclusively as a reference guide and not as a final scorecard. There are likely other factors to consider when beginning a new business venture such as who you might go into business with, geographical locations, and others. But these categories should give you a solid framework and better ensure you align your chosen hustle with your Life Vision.

Tips for Completing an Evaluation

- ▶ Add a column for each business opportunity you are looking to evaluate.
- ▶ Assign numbers 0 to 5 for each category and opportunity. Be sure to confirm the validity of your answers.
- ▶ As necessary, customize your scoring based on your particular situation. For example, starting a law firm if you are already a successful attorney requires much less work than if you haven't even applied for law school yet. Add other metrics that are important to you (geography, spousal support, operating costs versus launch costs, probability of success, etc.).
- ▶ Use the scoring and totals column for general reference, not for hard-lined decision making.
- ▶ Talk through the evaluation with others who have been successful in that industry.

FIGURE 4.1 Evaluating Your Side Hustle Options

(EXAMPLE)

Scoring Values:
? = Unknown, 0 = Not Viable, 1 = Least Favorable, 2 = Unfavorable, 2.5 = Neutral/Unknown, 3 = Favorable, 4 = Extremely Favorable, 5 = Already Accomplished
Special Note: These numbers are generic and will adjust based on an individual's capital, experience, goals, etc.

	ORIGINAL IDEA	REAL ESTATE (RENTAL)	FREELANCE (PHOTOGRAPHY)	FREELANCE (CONSULTING)	NETWORK MARKETING	REAL ESTATE (AGENT)	SMALL FRANCHISE	AFFILIATE MARKETING
Launch Costs	?	1	4	4	4	4	2	4
Scalability	?	2	2	2.5	3	3	2	2
Probability of "Success"	?	3	2	3	2.5	3	4	3
Passive Income	?	4	2	2	2.5	2.5	4	2
Quality Mentorship	?	2	2	2	3	3	4	1
Expertise Needed	?	2.5	4	3	4	3	3	3
Ongoing Risk	?	2	4	4	4	3	3	4
Sellable Asset	?	5	2	2	1	2	3	2
Time Frame for "Success"	?	2	3	3	2.5	3	2.5	2.5
TOTALS	?	23.5	25	25.5	26.5	26.5	27.5	23.5

Additional Notes:
1. In general, buying real estate will require more capital than becoming a real estate agent. However, if you are taking over your uncle's rental property at a large discount or investing sweat equity to acquire ownership, then the preceding numeric value may change. If you are looking to do some freelance accounting and have been a CPA for 20 years, your expertise needed is much more favorable than someone with no experience.

2. "Success" is defined by you and how your side hustle synergizes with your Life Vision. Someone who defines success as an extra $1,000/month cash that doesn't need to be passive in nature will find many of the preceding examples have more favorable success probabilities than someone who defines success as $100,000/year in progressive-passive or passive income.

FIGURE 4.1 Evaluating Your Side Hustle Options

(BLANK)

Scoring Values:
? = Unknown, **0** = Not Viable, **1** = Least Favorable, **2** = Unfavorable, **2.5** = Neutral/Unknown, **3** = Favorable, **4** = Extremely Favorable, **5** = Already Accomplished

	ORIGINAL IDEA:	OPTION 1:	OPTION 2:	OPTION 3:
Launch Costs				
Scalability				
Probability of "Success"				
Passive Income				
Quality Mentorship				
Expertise Needed				
Ongoing Risk				
Sellable Asset				
Time Frame for "Success"				
TOTALS				

Example: In general, buying a manufacturing company requires larger capital than, let's say, starting a real estate agency. However, if you have been helping your uncle run his manufacturing company for several years, he may be willing to work you into ownership or equity, sell you the business with some type of loan to be paid over the course of several years, or if the company is in distress sell to you at a discounted price. Figure 4.1 includes a blank evaluation chart.

— — —

Keep in mind, whichever vehicle, product, system, or platform (original or otherwise) you choose, seek out other individuals who have already created success, and *sit at their feet*. Get humble, they have already *freaking* done it (reread Chapter 3 if you need a reminder). And even if you are *inventing* the wheel, speaking to other successful inventors should prove highly beneficial.

Also, on tandemconsulting.co we have several recommended resources including an assessment for identifying your ideal side hustle options. Many of these systems often come with some sort of evaluation process of their own that can provide you added perspectives.

Next up, let's start drilling into some of the more tactical mindset and life decisions side hustlers need to make to grow a business in a sustainable way. We call these decisions and your way of living your *Lifeset*.

CHAPTER 5

Establishing a Solid Lifeset

Tell me how you use your spare time, and how you spend your money, and I will tell you where and what you will be in ten years from now.
—Napoleon Hill

Mindset: A person's way of *thinking* and their *opinions*.

Lifeset: A person's way of *living* and their *choices*.

As discussed in Chapter 3, your mindset is the primary driver for your success and that mindset is most deeply impacted by the WHO, but how it plays out in your choices and everyday living is what we call your Lifeset.

"All you have to do is put your mind to it." So untrue! Yes, of course, when you set your mind to a side hustle, you are focusing your attention and thoughts on it. But thoughts and mindset are not "doing." You need action. You cannot just plan, you must *live out your* plan and also need *follow-through*—but it needs to be the correct action and correct follow-through. Many people fail to apply proper mindset, as it gets lost in translation when taking action and applying it in their lives. This is precisely why when we mentor other side hustlers, we advise them to begin looking at the results their mindset is producing, their Lifeset.

We can provide countless examples of those ready to side hustle, coming to us for advice or mentorship, but when their job is shaky, their finances are upside down, and their relationships are on the rocks, what real concrete business-building power moves can they actually make? Many people may understand a mindset principle conceptually, but it's not reflected in their choices, leaving them without firm footing or a strong foundation to build upon.

You can categorize Lifeset into many different pillars in your life such as health, spiritual, relational, financial, and so on. There are ample books on each of these areas and we recommend making them all a priority. However, for the sake of this book, and when it comes to side hustling, we want to invest time into these two pillars: your career and your finances. Without making quality choices in these two categories, your foundation always remains unsteady, making it difficult to build that bodacious side hustle and manifest your dream life. Pillars are used in architecture for support, and when you have a stable career and strong personal finances, you can properly fund and support your side hustle in *a sustainable way*, and vice versa—creating a synergistic cycle.

To build wealth beyond the day job requires some form of investing. Investing time, money, and education (which often costs both). You also have to be willing to embrace some level of *risk* that it may not pay off. This requires an elevation of one's Lifeset; however, most people don't have close exposure to people living out the decisions and choices required to play at *such an elevated level*. Recall that without the WHO, a real example, it is difficult to piecemeal this together. This chapter is designed to help you build out the most relevant elements of a strong Lifeset, and as you seek out the WHO, your chances of your success radically improve.

Fortunately, you don't have to start out with an immaculate Lifeset in any particular category. We have empowered many people to evolve in these key areas and have watched their careers and personal finances make massive leaps forward. We want to share these fundamental lessons with you now.

Winning in Your Career *and* Side Hustle(s)

We have seen scores of individuals fail in their side hustle because of a job, career, or other income-related challenges. Ironically, many people are building a side hustle to replace their job income, but the first thing most side hustlers move to the back burner when they have a career challenge is . . . their side hustle. Despite the millions of people talking about the value of a side hustle, we have yet to encounter *any content* that specifically speaks to this challenge or provides real hard-hitting content and advice. This section provides you with specific Lifeset choices and examples you can implement immediately.

One of the many perks of having a side hustle (or hustles) is that you don't have to feel the need to put an overwhelming amount of pressure on your job. Once you have created a business of your own, your job no longer holds the responsibility of having to "complete you" or fill *all* of your emotional and financial needs. Having a side hustle gave us the freedom to look for a plan A that paid us well enough to generate extra cash to fund our side hustles, and provide us the flexibility we needed.

10 Tips for Winning in Both Your Career and Side Hustle

1. **Find an industry or role that provides flexibility.** We took roles in job sectors that were either standard banking hours or remote roles allowing us the freedom to run appointments for our side hustles. We cannot overstate the value of this. Had we taken jobs that buttoned us down tight for 50-plus hours a week, we would likely still be stuck there, too busy with our jobs to build a side hustle and create independence!

2. **Get paid as much as you can—assuming it doesn't seriously limit your capacity to run your side hustles.** Over the years, we have generally advised people to take the promotion or the pay raise, *but* we have also advised many people to *decline promotions.* Sometimes an extra $5,000 or $10,000 wasn't worth the stress or increased time investment that would pull them away from developing their side adventures and building wealth.

3. **Maintain integrity in your job role.** Don't take a job that has a clear conflict with your other ventures, and always perform the responsibilities as assigned to you. You don't want to sacrifice your honor to run a side hustle outside of your job. If there is a clear conflict, take this into consideration at the interview stage, consider switching roles, or perhaps put a temporary pause on your business activity.

4. **Go early or stay late.** We generally recommend going in early. This often gives you access to your boss, a jump on the day, and the ability to depart at closing time *sharp*, and go crush your side hustle.

5. **When you're at your job, be focused and productive.** Don't waste excessive time at the water coolers and the coffee pots of the corporate world. *Do not invest a lot of time complaining* about your job, the company, your coworkers, or your clients. In general, complaining is extremely unproductive and doesn't serve the greater good. We found if we put our heads down and stayed focused on our roles at work and the things we could control, we were substantially more productive than our counterparts.

6. **Work for competence and success—but establish boundaries for the time you invest in your job.** Deliver quality, good work. Make sure your boss and clients are happy. At the same time, you don't need to break any company world records. We were OK to invest up to 45 hours a week (as necessary) into our careers, but not 60 or 70. We had other assets to build and were interested in developing *wealth*, not just collecting extra kudos at the office. *It requires immense discipline not to get swept up in the culture and grind of your job environment.* Your managers and coworkers are likely one-sport athletes, but you have to think of yourself differently, and when the evenings, weekends, or lunch hours strike, be able to make a sharp pivot in a completely different direction.

7. **Learn how to *manage* your manager.** We always wanted our managers to realize we were on their team. We are not advising you to brown-nose—but make sure to let the captain of the team know you're a team player and will do what it takes to support them. Your boss needs to know, if you've been handed a project or clientele, it will be *handled*—bottom line. Understand your boss's priorities and underlying goals so you can help them. Our goal was to be the lowest-maintenance but highest-performing direct reports our managers had. As our side hustles grew, we didn't need to have the top numbers at work, but we never complained or had personality issues. Their ROI on us was going to be solid. In turn, our bosses came to trust us; so if we wanted to leave early, work from home, or needed some extra time off, it was a nonissue.

Craig here. One year, instead of requesting an additional raise, I asked for an extra week of *unpaid* vacation (thanks for the tip, Dad). My manager wasn't willing to do so *above* the table, but he was *below* the table. Comically, the same year I received the highest annual merit raise in our division. Post-review my boss laughed and shared, "Well, Craig, I can give you a bigger raise because 9 percent of not much (in reference to my salary) is still, well . . . *not much*."

That extra week of vacation and flexibility gave us the peace of mind and freedom to *hammer* our side hustles in the evenings and weekends. Keep in mind, as someone building assets and businesses outside your job, your time is more valuable (monetarily) and has a greater opportunity cost. A day off or even an hour longer lunch meant a chance to buy our way out of a job *faster*.

8. **Work your freaking face off.** After writing several chapters in this book, we realized how little we have discussed our work ethic, or more important, the work ethic that necessitates building a successful side hustle. Now if you are smarter than us, are leveraging better systems than us, or were straight up dealt pocket rockets on your first hand at the table of entrepreneurship (poker reference for "extremely lucky"), you won't have to do the following.

   But personally, we worked 20- to 50-hour workweeks *in addition* to our jobs, through much of our twenties. Few business owners at high levels of success don't work their guts out at some point in their journey. We don't apologize for it, and I'm not saying you will or need to. A good rule of thumb if you are looking to create real momentum from your side hustle: for every hour we put into someone else's business, we were willing to invest an hour into our own.

Keep in mind, being a *successful* entrepreneur is not a right, it is a privilege you earn with your toil, sweat, and willingness to learn and make smart, sometimes difficult decisions. We feel confident if you execute on much of the advice listed above, your capacity to crush your side hustle will improve.

Financial Management

To run a side hustle, you need capital (aka money). How much, how often, and where that money comes from varies, but most side hustlers fund their business via their personal savings or surplus cash flow from their job. Therefore, optimizing your personal finances supports your side hustle in three critical ways:

1. It supplies your side hustle with the capital and funding necessary to launch and continue in a sustainable way.
2. It disciplines and educates you to manage your money properly, so you can in turn manage your business's finances well. If you cannot manage a $60,000 salary well, how will you possibly manage the cash flow of a $600,000 business?
3. Many aspiring side hustlers do not realize that banks and other lenders provide business loans *based primarily off the proprietor's personal finances and credit scores, not the businesses.* Banks are unlikely to lend to a small business if the owner has few assets or marginal credit.

> **Essentially, your personal finances and side hustle's finances will be married for *years* to come, potentially until death due you part.**

Because of the importance of having all your personal finance ducks in a row, we want to take our time here and provide you as much value as we can through detailed and poignant Lifeset examples and tips. This section focuses primarily on your personal financial management for the preceding reasons. Please note, we build on this foundation and discuss how to raise additional capital for your business more specifically in Chapter 10.

We have met many smart people who make poor financial decisions due to a lack of either education, inexperience, or a low FEQ (financial emotional quotient). Learning how to optimize your resources provides you the best chance to invest in your side hustle.

Some disclaimers: We are *not* financial advisors, certified public accountants (CPAs), or attorneys. Craig does have degrees in finance and economics, a concentration in financial planning, and 15-plus years of experience in commercial finance and banking with some major financial institutions. As a former commercial credit analyst, risk analyst, and business banker, he has likely seen the guts of more financial statements than many surgeons have seen the actual guts of humans. On top of that, together we have scaled multiple businesses, assisted many aspiring entrepreneurs, and advised business owners and entrepreneurs how to run and financially manage their firms across many different industries. Most important, we earned the right to step away from our traditional jobs and control our time *because we managed both our revenues and expenses effectively.*

We will *not* focus on how to invest a $100,000 and turn it into $500,000 or how to short sell shares in Blockbuster. That's not our expertise (although we certainly have our opinions). Instead, we *focus* on how to help you make smart Lifeset decisions and put yourself in the best position to *cash flow your life.*

People often come to us asking for financial advice—whether they should buy a particular car, put more money into their 401(k), or take an all-commission job with a higher-earning potential. The answer is: *it depends.*

It depends on your current state and your desired future state. What are you trying to accomplish? What is the destination? How does this decision impact your other assets or liabilities? What is your age, tax bracket, current debt? Be wary of anyone who is willing to dole out financial advice but doesn't understand (or even ask) these questions. The saying "free advice is worth what you paid for it" is often spot on—and unfortunately, "free" can actually be *extremely expensive.*

We recommend side hustlers get into the simple groove of making more than they spend. If this is a large problem, we provide you with some basic guidelines, but there are additional books that go into much greater detail, like *The Total Money Makeover* by Dave Ramsey. These resources are particularly important if you are consistently upside down in consumer debt, as you likely have deeper systemic issues in your thinking.

Fortunately, Craig grew up in a family of relatively pragmatic and frugal engineers who helped him understand the importance of not spending money you do not have, and from a savings perspective, this has served us well. Unfortunately, many people are not taught this discipline growing up. The best thing you can do is learn it *now* and begin living it *now,* so your next generation has a good example.

However, if your goal is to build assets, businesses, or investments and step away from corporate America at an untraditional age, *just saving money alone* is likely not enough. You need to build on top of this foundational Lifeset to create wealth at a faster rate. As a result, your peers no longer become good markers of progress or the quality influence you need.

Step 1: Develop a Budget

The best way to know what direction to walk in next is to know where you want to go. The *next best* is to understand where you *are*. If you want to go to Chicago, should you go east or west? It depends if you live in Colorado or New York.

People often do not have a clean line of sight on their current financial situation. We have witnessed this firsthand as we have helped people from high school students to high-end income earners and entrepreneurs with their budgets.

> Burying your head in the sand doesn't make a hurricane go away. You need the *financial courage* to take a real look at what you've got and what you don't.

There are two fairly elementary components to assessing your financial health: a balance sheet and an income statement. A balance sheet is a snapshot in time of all your assets and liabilities. The income statement is a list of all your incomes and expenses over a period of time. We generally recommend running a budget based on your monthly spending but basing these numbers off annual averages.

It is mind-numbing to us the level of detail people know about a professional sports team, their project at work, something in the political world, or the Kardashians, and yet have no idea how much money is in their 401(k) from their prior employer.

Figure 5.1 is a budgeting sheet that's relevant for most people who read this book. (You can also find this document for download at tandemconsulting.co.) There are more detailed budgeting worksheets, but it's important to use something that doesn't feel overwhelming or intimidating and to work on the numbers that are relevant to the level in which you operate.

FIGURE 5.1 **Personal Monthly Budget**

MONTHLY BUDGET

CASH FLOW SUMMARY	AMOUNT	NOTES
TOTAL INCOME	0.00	
TOTAL EXPENSES	0.00	
MONTHLY SURPLUS/DEFICIT	**0.00**	

INCOME/DEDUCTIONS		
Salary / Wages		
Tax Deductions		
401K / 403B Contributions		
Benefits / Other Deducations		
Interest Income		
Dividends		
Refunds / Reimbursements		
Business Income		
Real Estate Income		
Pension		
Misc.		
TOTAL	**0.00**	

DEBT EXPENSES	AMOUNT	NOTES
Mortgage		
Home Equity Line / 2nd Mortg.		
Auto		
Credit Card 1		
Credit Card 2		
Student Loan 1		
Student Loan 2		
Personal / Family Loan		
Accounts Payable / Other		
TOTAL	**0.00**	

EXPENSES	AMOUNT	NOTES
HOME		
Rent		
Home / Rental Insurance		
Electricity / Gas / Oil		
Water / Sewer / Trash		
Cable / Satellite / Internet		
Phone		
Furnishing / Appliances		
Lawn / Garden		
Maintenance / Improvements		
Other (Unlikely Zero)		
	0.00	
TRANSPORTATION		
Repairs / Maintenance		
Auto Insurance		
Fuel		
Parking / Public Transporation		
Registration / License		
	0.00	
DAILY LIVING		
Groceries		
Dining Out		
Childcare		
Clothing		
Cleaning / Supplies		
Salon / Barber / Pet / Misc.		
	0.00	
BUSINESS EXPENSES		
Travel Costs		
Marketing / Sales / Promotional		
Tools / Equipment / Supplies		
Licenses / Fees / Dues		
Other		
	0.00	
HEALTH		
Life / Health Insurance		
Gym Membership		
Doctors / Dentist Visits		
Medicine / Prescriptions		
	0.00	
ENTERTAINMENT / VACATION		
Airfare / Car Rental		
Accommodations		
Food / Beverages		
Sports / Outdoor		
Concerts / Plays / Movies		
Subscriptions: Netflix, Hulu, Etc..		
Parties / Hosting		
	0.00	
TOTAL MONTHLY EXPENSES	**0.00**	

Once you know where you stand financially and how you are cash flowing, and have taken an honest look at your real-life expenses, your debt structure, and what types of interest rates you may have, then you can decide how to apply your surplus cash or monthly cash flow.

Having a solid budget is one of the first steps in making major financial progress. If you don't know what you have or what you owe, you cannot assemble a good plan. Here are some key elements to consider:

1. In general, do you make more money than you spend? If not, how can you begin cutting back expenses or increasing your income right away? If you do cash flow, how can you optimize it?
2. If you have debt, what type of interest rates do you have and how can you pay this off or move to lower interest rates? If you have debt, *do not ignore it.* Look at it *directly* and put a plan together right away. Even small amounts of progress paying off debt creates important forward momentum.
3. If you have savings or other assets, you can use these to enhance your wealth. Make sure your assets are in the right financial buckets and managed by quality money managers you trust.
4. What are your financial goals? What is the proper timing to achieve those goals based on where you are now?

For many people, simply having a fully completed balance sheet and listing out their incomes and expenses is in and of itself 80 percent of the work. Of course, if you have internally labeled yourself as not a "numbers person," hiring someone else to go through this with you can be helpful.

Step 2: Earning *Income*

We believe if you are going to have a job, you should get the most leverage from it! Meaning, many people either don't make enough income, or their time is so buried in their job they don't have the freedom of flexibility to *create income* outside of their job, which is the point of a side hustle in the first place. Here are a couple challenging scenarios people may find themselves in that are not addressed in the prior section:

▸ **Being *underpaid* at your current job.** In this case your wage and skill sets would let you make more, but you haven't fought, pushed, worked hard enough, or demanded better pay or a more flexible role that puts you in pole position to crush your side hustle. In these scenarios you need to *step up and ask for it.* Not in a demanding way, but in a well-thought-out, smart, and confident way.

▶ **Assuming too much responsibility and work for the role you have.** Remember, *you don't have to be the superstar anymore; you just need to do good quality work.* There is a different set of goals for you. Learn how to manage your time, your boss, and your role more effectively so you can earn more flexibility, not just income.

▶ **You have not developed enough *skills or marketability* to acquire a role that sets your life up for foundational financial success.** Let's be honest, if you are working for $11/hour in the United States right now and trying to support a family or dependents, just paying your bills and managing life is likely a financial struggle. You are probably more focused on *survival* versus leveling up, because *life is expensive.* Carrie's favorite quote from the play *The Humans* is "Why does it cost so much to be a human being?" Many can relate to this sentiment, whether fleeting or chronic, and no doubt many individuals face significantly more barriers in regard to the constraints they must overcome. We acknowledge life is not always an equal playing field. However, as much as possible you have to fight to develop new skills, habits, mindset, and associations that can support you in a positive spiral upward. Work to access a distant relative, community leader, or religious organization that you think will give you exposure to their mindset. And in the interim, cut back on any unnecessary expenses as you push yourself into a new environment, school, or other certification program where you can upskill your abilities, hourly wage, salary, or marketability and get the cash flowing. We cannot always guarantee a victory, but you owe it to yourself to fight for it.

▶ **If necessary, get a part-time job or cash work to fund your side adventure; essentially, get a side hustle to fund the side hustle.** There are many ways to make extra cash—from having a garage sale, becoming a bartender, selling shoes on eBay, driving for Uber, and so on. Figure out what you have to do temporarily for cash so you don't have to give up on building a side hustle that can significantly impact your life.

Step 3: Managing *Expenses*

Overspending and living beyond one's means is a ubiquitous and systemic problem in our culture. We live in a consumer-based society that is constantly sending us subliminal and blatant messages that you are *not good* enough, *sexy* enough, or will not be *happy* unless you own the newest gadgets, nicest clothes, or fanciest car. Now, this is not to say we are against buying nice or even expensive things. But we have been relatively good about not buying fancy things, especially beyond our budget, solely to impress other people or to fulfill an emotional void.

Questions to Ask Yourself to Curb Overspending

- Is this the most valuable thing I could spend this money on?
- Does this purchase bring me closer to my/our family's Life Vision?
- When I purchased these items in the past, did it improve or hurt my self-image?
- Do I have the *financial strength* to afford this, and have I *earned* the right to this purchase?
- Would I or my loved ones feel more secure if this money was cash in our checking or savings account?
- Instead of spending this money, would I be happier if I invested it and had more in the future? (Consider, money invested now at a 10 percent rate of return will double in about 7 years and multiply by 10 times in 30 years.)

When people spend money they haven't earned yet, they sell themselves into financial bondage. They now must go to work for the next six months or *several years* just to pay for something they purchased today. This can be a painful cycle.

Example

Suppose you buy a *new* car for $25,000. You don't have the cash to pay up front, so you put down only $2,000 and finance the rest at 5 percent interest. Take a closer look at what the vehicle is actually going to cost you in Figure 5.2.

FIGURE 5.2 **Vehicle Purchase**

(Numbers are estimated based on standard costs.)

$25,000	Vehicle Purchase Price
$1,750	7% Sales Tax (varies by state)
$500	Fees (loan origin, title, registration, dealer, new plates, etc.)
–$2,000	Cash Down or Trade-In Credit
$25,250	Amount Financed
$2,000	$400 *Increase* of Annual Insurance Premium × 5 Years (est.)
$3,340	Total Interest Paid 5% × 5 Years
$2,000	Add Back Cash Down
$32,590	**TOTAL Cost of Vehicle**
$10,000	Est. Vehicle Value at 100,000 Miles (5 years × 20,000/year)
$22,590	LOST VALUE After 5 Years
$2,000	Est. Vehicle Value at 200,000 Miles (10 years × 20,000/year)
$30,590	LOST VALUE After 10 Years

So if at the financial outset of your life, the biggest purchase you are going to make is theoretically worth $25,000, but you are paying $32,000-plus, and after 5 years it is worth $10,000 and after 10 years it is worth $2,000? Minus the value you got from driving, you just blew $30,590. Now if you are worth $800,000 and make $200,000 a year, *go for it*. But if your net worth is $50,000, you just *blew over 60 percent of the entire net worth that it has taken your entire life to accumulate*.

On a salary of $60,000 and take-home of $50,000, you literally have to work nearly *8 months* of your life just to pay for a car that is worth almost nothing 10 years later. Now we are not anti-borrowing at all—it does provide a way to leverage the cash or assets you have—but if you do overspend on something, consider a home, land, or an education, as these typically provide or hold stronger value over time.

Homes also are taxed and require insurance but a $300,000 home after 10 years is usually worth *around* $300,000, not $3,000. *Think about it.* Buying an expensive vehicle is generally a cruel thing to do to your balance sheet and financial future. Of course, these are general numbers. Sometimes people get all uppity with us and say, "Well, my truck will be worth more than that after five years." Great. The math is still inaccurate. If you would have bought a $10,000 used sedan with 60,000 miles (under warranty until 100,000) and put down $2,000, total cost of your taxes, depreciation, and interest are significantly less.

> **Until you have earned and saved $20,000, totally unencumbered in cash, you don't truly understand the** *value of $20,000.*

It is a completely different experience to write the check in cash because you have created the savings. If you have never created it, you don't know how hard (or seemingly easy) it is. Interestingly, when you actually have money available to you and understand how hard you worked to generate it, you know what you truly value by how you spend it. *One way we vote on our values is with our money.* We acknowledge this mindset of "if you don't have the money, don't spend it" is considered contrarian by much of society, but so is building a successful business.

We are not saying you should or should not buy a quality vehicle. Buy whatever kind of vehicle you want. We simply want to empower you to *think for yourself.* This goes back to values; if you have young children and live in the mountains, and acquiring a safe vehicle is heavily valued, invest as necessary.

Now that you have our line of thinking you can apply this same mindset to other things you purchase. If you make $25/hour and you buy something for $500, you are also paying the sales tax on it, losing the time value of the money it could make on the market, and if you finance it, you are spending quite a bit more than $550. That's 22 or 23 hours of *your life you just traded for the "thing" you now own.*

A few common problematic areas we see for many people are listed as follows. Please challenge yourself to consider if any of these categories are causing you unnecessary pain and if those resources could be better allocated toward building a side hustle!

- Vehicles, expensive clothes, jewelry, dining out
- Alcohol (in particular at bars, restaurants, etc.), junk food, cell phones, TVs, gadgets
- Cars, expensive vacations, concerts, sporting events, subscriptions (be wary as these are *residual* expenses!)
- More home than you need, and expensive toys such as snowmobiles, boats, motorcycles, etc.

Many struggle to see how they will supply the investment money or manage the operating cost of starting a business. **When you minimize costs like the preceding, you may find you have enough money to fund your business.** As you review your budget, continue to look for other opportunities. Perhaps it's large items like rent or a car or smaller bills like your cell phone, internet, or auto insurance. Shop these services every couple of years to keep your current providers honest and competitive.

Managing Credit Cards

We run everything through our credit cards because of the rewards we receive and the average 40-day payment delay on the bill lets us keep extra cash on hand. We pay every bill off in full and do not pay fees or interest. If using a credit card to pay certain bills like car payments, tuition, and auto insurance requires an extra fee, we pay using cash or direct withdrawal from our checking. We don't generally advise paying extra percentage points.

However, if historically you've had a problem overspending, then we *do not* recommend using credit cards. Until you have the self-discipline to properly manage them, you should not use them. If you charge it, you should have the cash in the bank to pay for it.

Unless an emergency, *do not carry ongoing credit card balances* and make sure all your payments are made on time or your interest rate and fees will go through the ceiling without you knowing. Also, if you do make a mistake and forget to pay a bill, credit card companies often waive many "annual fees" or even interest if you push hard enough. Fifty bucks here or there adds up. Again, this could be what you need to start your side hustle.

Owning Your Personal Credit Score

Building up a solid credit score can be helpful in many ways, especially when you do want to borrow money in the future, personally, or for your business! The best way to do this is to have a credit card, mortgage, or home equity line of credit and use them responsibly.

A good credit score usually involves having *a lot of credit you do not use*. For example, if you have a credit card with a $20,000 credit limit, but only borrow $1,000, you have $19,000 in available credit. The credit-scoring algorithms love this— along with those who pay their bills in full and on time.

If you do have bad credit you can acquire a free copy of your credit report and start working to pay off anything that may be late or dispute anything inaccurate! Go back to your budget and consider picking up another job or other forms of generating cash to accelerate paying these items swiftly if your side hustle isn't ready to support this yet.

Managing Other Personal Debt

If you have a lot of personal debt, it can be overcome. You likely need to make some changes in your habits and educate yourself on better money management, but we have guided countless individuals to get out of $20,000, $50,000, or even a $100,000 of debt.

On debt you do carry, like anything, *shop around*. Identify the best price but do watch out for excessive loan fees. If you are unsure if you should make a change, you can always *dollarize* your savings, meaning determine how much savings a new interest rate saves you in actual dollars.

We don't want to run through infinite different scenarios; we want you to understand this mindset so you can *self-prescribe* in the future and make stronger Lifeset decisions.

Step 4: Building *Wealth*

Building wealth requires an entirely different mindset, and corresponding Lifeset, compared to simply making money and managing expenses. To *create wealth* in your twenties or thirties takes an elevated game beyond what most of society does or teaches. Since creating wealth is often a primary purpose for building a side hustle, let's take a deeper dive here.

The average twentieth-century game plan for a financially successful life was to get a good job, work hard, live humbly, and save. This works relatively well if you make a solid income, live humbly, and want to spend 40 years in a full-time career. But this plan also has several limitations and risks—we refer to this as the "pile" theory. Save enough money through your 401(k)s, or over the course of your life, then *eventually* you will have your $250,000, $1 million, or $2 million saved that you need to live comfortably. Combine this with social *in*security and you should be all set! If you are looking to bunt or only plan to get to first base in the game of finances, this is a relatively sound plan. But a few questions to ask yourself:

1. **Will the pile be enough?** The average *current life expectancy* in the United States is 79 years old. Of course, many live much longer since the average includes all causes of mortality. Where was medical science 40 or 50 years ago, and where will it be further into the twenty-first century? With the exponential growth rate of technology, planning to go out at 80 may not be conservative or wise. If you live to 90 or 100 and the markets dip at the wrong time or Social Security gets cut or reduced, *what is your plan?* Do you want to put extra financial stress on yourself, pick up a part-time gig at 85, or burden other loved ones?

2. **Is the pile *too big*?** Certainly a better side of the equation to be on, but who wants to work hard their whole life, limit their activities, only to realize too late they could have taken more vacations, given more to their grandchildren or children while alive, and enjoyed that giving? Most want to leave some money for their loved ones and children, but what is the right amount? Too much and they may become spoiled or disincentivized to do anything with their lives; not enough and they have to go through a similar hardship as you may have.

3. **How will my pile be valued 40 years from now?** Inflation, health issues, artificial intelligence (AI), globalization, and other automation all make it difficult to manage to this challenge. What will the dollar, euro, or rupee be worth in 40 years? How much

will intensive medical care cost? What does health care even look like in 2050? All these variables present a unique challenge when you have only *one* lump sum pile of money without other forms of income.

Our solution: Roll with the pile theory *and* hedge against these challenges by also building assets that produce genuine cash flow (side hustles). If you own real estate, a business, or other forms of cash-producing assets that can generate ongoing revenue, then you have diversified and built a financial instrument that oftentimes hedges against inflation. In addition, you can usually sell the asset, or will the asset or cash flow to loved ones.

Ultimately, there only two reasonable options to building wealth. So let's look at them both directly—as they are your *only* options.

Option 1: Systematic Savings and Investment

We cannot impress upon anyone enough the value of executing on both building your own business and systematically saving (aka the pile theory). You may have seen similar charts like Figure 5.3, but we encourage you to really look at this clearly and understand the magnitude of how saving a few thousand now can turn into *tens of thousands* in the future.

FIGURE 5.3 **Investment Projections with Compound Interest Estimates**

(compounded annually)

		10 Years	30 Years	30 Years	30 Years
INTEREST RATE	INITIAL INVESTMENT	NO ADDITIONAL CONTRIBUTION	NO ADDITIONAL CONTRIBUTION	$100 MONTHLY CONTRIBUTION	$200 MONTHLY CONTRIBUTION
7%	$5,000	$9,836	$38,061	$151,414	$264,767
10%	$5,000	$12,969	$87,247	$284,640	$482,033
7%	$20,000	$39,343	$152,245	$265,598	$378,951
10%	$20,000	$51,875	$348,988	$546,381	$743,774

Imagine if after five years of losing $20,000 on the preceding vehicle purchase example you had instead invested that money and contributed

$200 per month (some of which you could get from lower insurance rates). You would potentially create over $743,000 of investments 30 years from now. *That's just ONE purchase.* If this doesn't motivate you to manage your money in a more responsible way, we don't know what will.

There are many online calculators you can use to run your own estimates, but a very simple one can be found on investor.gov.

Do not, we repeat, *do not* underestimate the value of systematic savings.

Option 2: Building a Business

The challenge with relying solely on investing is you need a lot of capital, time, skill, or luck. If you don't have some or all of these and you truly want to build wealth, welcome to the world of business ownership. However, business ownership has its own form of investment, both in time and monetarily.

We have always contributed money to our 401(k)s when we had jobs and now to our 401(k)s as being self-employed. We have also played the IRA Roth game—but we didn't *stop* there! Hence, again, the value of a *side hustle.*

Remember, to build wealth beyond the day job requires some form of investing. Investing in retirement and savings funds are normalized, but investing in a business that doesn't always provide short-term returns is abnormal. Coming from middle-class backgrounds, we had to fight the mindset of *saving less* to spend more—essentially learning how to consider our "spending" on our side hustles as *investments*. From small things such as association dues, taking business trips, or investing in inventory, **strong business owners see what they are purchasing as an eventual asset or something that will pay them more in the future for what the cost is today.** For many aspiring side hustlers, this is a difficult mindset shift, and one they never make.

There are scores of examples. We can both recall booking flights in our first year of business ownership (when they were not producing income yet). We were both making around $30,000 in our jobs at that point. Booking $300 flights and $40 for luggage *did* feel crazy, as we were dropping 1 percent of our annual income on flights with no guarantees of creating any revenue from our trips. But if we hadn't been willing to make these types of investments, we never would have been able to build what we have today.

We chose to live humbly and make our basic retirement contributions, and we were willing to essentially invest everything else into our side hustles. We funded our businesses instead of financing sporting outings, cable, big-screen TVs, cars, five-dollar mochas, or fancy vacations. In fact, we didn't even own a TV for a decade (until our first business exceeded $1 million in revenue). This annoyed the daylights out of our parents and relatives . . . let's just say no one was ever planning to watch the big game at C&C's house! It's unrealistic to expect uncommon results in life if you don't do uncommon things.

In addition, for several years of our twenties we did not max out our Roth IRA contributions. We remember our financial planner (who is a couple years older than us) giving us a hard time about this. So we asked if he had maxed out *his* Roth contributions during the first couple years building his financial planning business, to which he replied: "No." He does well now and so do we, but the businesses we built produce *significantly more* income than the $12,000 we missed out on from a handful of Roth contributions.

Now, being willing to invest money into your side hustle is the *first* step. *When* and *how* to invest that money in your business is the next level of thinking, which we discuss in upcoming chapters.

CHAPTER 6

The Inside Job of Building a Side Hustle

Nothing will work unless you do.
—Maya Angelou

Success is not as external as most think. It is more often inside work. People who view their success as a separate part of themselves may not experience growth in the ways they plan. Who you are, what you believe about yourself and your capacity, and how you align all of that with your core values is known as *self-image*.

In addition, you are unlikely to ever build a business that exceeds your self-image—or be able to lead people who have a stronger self-image than you do.

> **Self-image is not just one ingredient of the side hustle; *it is the magic ingredient*.**

Self-image runs deep in one's inner-world and affects one's relationship with the outer-world. It impacts every area of life: from the salary you do (or don't) negotiate, the people you network with (or don't have the guts to network with), the sale you ask for (or don't ask for), and the boundaries you keep (or don't keep) with people. It's reflected in your overall approach to life and business and has a strong correlation to the *results* you pull in as a side hustler. This is why we are dedicating an entire chapter to this topic.

Whether you want to create an extra $2,000 a month of income from your side hustle or circumnavigate the globe on your personal yacht with your ukulele-playing children, you are working to create results beyond where you are. The question becomes, does your self-image, your belief in your capacity and your value, match that Life Vision or is there a misalignment between what you want to create and what you believe you actually can?

Which brings two options:

1. Pretend like you never read this chapter and maintain your current self-image level. Continue to chip away and focus on strategies, products, or new ideas—when the root issue remains *you*.
2. Choose to go on the offensive and attack growing your self-image. This takes both courage and work, but the results won't just change your end game; they can change how you interact and engage with the world on a micro, day-to-day level. The work changes you, whereby changing your business, influence, and even happiness.

A side hustle was never just a side hustle for us, which is why we chose option 2. As we self-reflected, got honest, and worked through areas of weakness or self-limiting beliefs, building a business carried more significance in our lives. If you are also up for option 2, use the following methods as self-development boosters to grow your self-image:

1. Adopt a growth mindset and learn to attach your self-image to beliefs that are antifragile.
2. Take action and use experiential learning to develop new skills.
3. Evolve your ability to communicate through repetition, self-analysis and study.
4. Grow your leadership to grow your self-image and vice versa. They are symbiotic.

Adopting and Developing a Growth Mindset

According to Carol Dweck, author of *Mindset: The New Psychology of Success*, a growth mindset is "based on the belief that your basic qualities are things you can cultivate through your efforts." Developing a growth mindset is a foundational tool for expanding your self-concept. Dweck explains, "Although people may differ in every which way in their initial talents and aptitudes, interests and temperaments, everyone can change and grow through application and experience." A growth mindset as a side hustler is acknowledging that you are way more multidimensional than your job title.

The binary measure of the pass/fail, successful/unsuccessful label is problematic as you start a business, because initially you may not see yourself, your skills, or your ability beyond the small confines of the job title you brought with you. You may not see yourself executing as a business owner yet.

So how are you going to act like a business owner if you don't identify as someone who is? You won't. You need to create a new headspace and rewrite the way you think about yourself. We challenge you to take a step back and begin identifying yourself as a growth-oriented adjective versus a static job title or noun, an adjective that is more durable, resilient, or adventurous. So, the "losses" don't become permanent setbacks for your self-image but opportunities for growth.

Common scenarios for those who have never built a business before may include weak self-talk, telling yourself you are deficient in something, or that you are up against unbeatable obstacles. For instance:

- "I don't have enough experience or credibility to network with highly successful entrepreneurs."
- "I am not high tech, and I don't understand social media, so I'm just going to keep doing what I've always done."
- "I've never been an effective public speaker, so I am going to take more of a background role."

Age and experience are easy justifications for why people shouldn't stretch themselves and learn new things. Be the person who proves them wrong and set new standards for what successful people look like. In doing so you will be a pioneer for others to see how their own limiting beliefs are unwarranted. Remember, Toni Morrison didn't publish her first novel until she was 39, Vera Wang hadn't entered the design scene until age 40, and Samuel L. Jackson performed in small-scale roles until his big breakthrough performance at age 43. Had they not embraced a lifelong mentality of being learners, they would have missed out on what ended up being stratospheric success.

We can dissect another common example of a fixed mindset: "My business partner is much stronger at X aspect of business, so I'll just let them run the show in that department." There is definitely power in identifying strengths and designating roles and responsibilities, but we also can't be too quick to limit our ability to evolve. Carrie here. I can think of countless areas of expertise where Craig had stronger business skills initially. He came from a commercial banking background, which justified me thinking I should defer to him in many areas. Fortunately, I didn't have a fixed mindset and worked on developing those skills over time. Had I not done so, I would still be bound by those limitations today and wouldn't have grown my entrepreneurial self-image. Not only was I able to acquire new strengths and skills, but I also can now bring my own natural flair and authority to the game, and ultimately, can change the game. When you take something and add your spin or your lens to it, you don't just grow it, you evolve it.

> **Understand that everything in business is a skill set, and skill sets can be learned. If you have faith in your capacity to learn new skills, you will.**

Top Tips for Overcoming a Fixed Mindset

1. **Take stock of limiting beliefs you have.** Identifying specific thought processes that are holding you back makes it easier to change your thinking.
2. **What do you attach your self-image to?** Are you anchoring your confidence in achievements? Failures? Timelines? Are these stories or beliefs serving you well? Wealth, looks, and material goods can be lost or taken away. As discussed, attach your self-image to things that are antifragile.

3. **Actively seek out opportunities for self-improvement.** Be intentional and deliberate in your personal growth, as it doesn't just happen to you. You seek it out and work at it.

4. **Explore a wide range of learning approaches.** Be open minded; you never know what environment or style will click until you experience it.

5. **Celebrate what you are learning—especially early on.** Being results driven is important, and they will come, but we don't recommend attaching your self image to them.

6. **Take more risks and be willing to embrace manageable failures.** You have to fail to succeed, so go find different ways to keep challenging yourself and growing new muscles. It might mean asking an acquaintance if they can give you a warm introduction to a key player in your industry, following up with an existing client to capture a repeat sale, or being more deliberate with your follow-through when you are not entirely sure how the potential client will respond. The list of ways you can put yourself out there without a guarantee of "success" is infinite, but knowing that these "failures" are not going to break you is key.

Use Personal Branding to Grow Your Self-Image *and* Your Side Hustle

We believe entrepreneurship is one of the best forms of self-development. When people begin to think of you as someone who is growth-oriented and willing to improve themselves, your branding will improve. If you do this through honesty and good quality work, your self-image will grow also.

For example, when you think of someone you know, for most people, only their top two or three attributes pop into your mind. The human brain naturally oversimplifies things as it's very difficult to truly process humans in all our infinite complexity. If you don't believe us, randomly pick a few people you know. How does your brain categorize those individuals? Your boss? Your coworker? Your cousin?

So *our big question for you is what three words come to other's minds when they think of you?* Not just what do you want them to think about you, but what do they actually think when your name comes up? Have you ever really thought about this? If you have the courage, you can poll some of your closest family and friends—and encourage them to be genuine! It may be some of the most important work you will do.

How people view us impacts how much *perceived value* they believe we can bring, whether it's launching a big marketing campaign for their company, managing someone's finances, or dog sitting. Your branding impacts if someone will hire you, do business with you, refer you, or even have positive thoughts when your name comes to mind.

So begin working on your own personal branding *yesterday.* Start by embracing a growth mindset to evolve who you are, and those three attributes that come to others' minds about you will begin to grow also. We take a deeper dive on this topic later on in Chapter 10 when we discuss how to translate your authentic personal brand into your business brand.

Experiential Learning

There is a massive underemphasis on experiential learning (i.e., learning in the field) in the twenty-first century. While memorizing data and other facts can be helpful, such rote knowledge does not carry the weight it once did prior to the days of Google and the internet. The traditional educational system, although making strides, has not been able to keep up with this change. If you grew up with standard institutionalized learning, it can be *very* tricky to transition to a learn-by-doing approach. When you take action and do work experientially, you are more likely to create real growth and change, instead of gathering information exclusively from reading and understanding something on an intellectual level. The conundrum for many is when they don't have experience, they lack the self-image to take steps forward. So if you don't have complete footing on an idea, a task, a mindset, or a venture you're taking on, you want to make a large-scale paradigm shift about how you acquire knowledge so intimidation of failure does not get in your way.

True growth lies in being on the fringe of your competency. This means you have to be willing to risk feeling or looking incompetent to develop a new skill. If you are always feeling competent, you probably aren't pushing yourself hard enough.

How do you put yourself on the fringe of competency? You put in effort and develop a strong work habit. Sounds easy, but most people are freakin' awesome at psyching themselves out and quitting before they ever really start. Why? Out of fear of the dreaded *F word*. Failure. As a function, most never even step onto the starting blocks and develop the necessary work habit, because they don't have enough self-trust or belief that it's OK to fail. It's part of starting a side hustle—you want to own the scrapes and bruises. Learn how to accept the discomfort of failure by embracing the suck. Most people unfortunately suck at sucking. But since it's unavoidable, let's learn how to be effective at it!

How to Not Suck at Sucking

1. **Embrace the power of failing *forward*.** When you accept blunders as being inevitable, and are still willing to walk the path, it strengthens your self-image. You've not only identified yourself as a learner but you're also living it and gaining intel along the way.

2. **Reflect on areas of your life where you already have success.** No doubt you created progress and forward motion in those areas if you had a growth mindset around the work. Your wins, oftentimes small, potentially didn't come at the speed or scale you may have anticipated, *but you moved the needle* because you believed that if you did more and thought less good things would develop. This belief, or essentially faith, is required growing your side hustle!

3. **Action undercuts insecurity with enough repetition.** It's not magic. Life rewards action. You could read this book a dozen times, but until you get out and start facing the uncomfortable work such as networking with people, public speaking, or closing a sale, you remain capped. Until you make your move, you remain latent potential, meaning the potential *exists* but it is *not yet actualized*.

4. **Focus on "one foot in front of the other" as you create progressive growth.** This relieves pressure and helps narrow in one's attention to the bite-size manageable tasks at hand. These feel more achievable as you trim down the more intimidating, long-term, peripheral tasks (that need to happen at some point but not right now). The effect incremental growth has on your self-image is so powerful as you start hacking away at the work instead of letting a mountain of intimidation accrue.

Miguel Ruiz, author of *The Four Agreements*, states:

> Action is about living fully. Inaction is the way that we deny life. Inaction is sitting in front of the television every day for years because you are afraid to be alive and to take the risk of expressing what you are. Expressing what you are is taking action. You can have many great ideas in your head, but what makes the difference is the action. Without action upon an idea, there will be no manifestation, no results, and no reward.

Let's apply this action-anchored approach to your side hustle. Grab a pen, paper, *and* your calendar!

Write down the top three areas of your side hustle in which you need to take more action. What ways are you not effectively or consistently investing in? Many people think they are taking action when they are actually just in preparation mode. Note, when you are chronically in prep mode, you frankly get *overly* good at preparation.

Do a strong gap analysis on where more action needs to be taken to get you closer to your goals. Write down three sub-steps you can take to the action items you've identified above. Create deadlines, and put those task items into your calendar with a set date and time. For example, do you have a coaching business but struggle to book enough clients? Go do more networking to increase your sample size of potential clients! Bump up your time investment to prioritize networking; go to in-person networking events, join a professional networking group, or start making connections virtually.

Stop "no showing" yourself! People are often exceptionally accountable to following through on obligations with other human beings but shortcut their own internal agreements. When was the last time you "no showed" a friend, family member, or professional acquaintance? Now how casual are you with your own habits on your calendar?

Treat yourself like a top-priority client in terms of your accountability.

> **Many people book their calendar with a black Sharpie when it includes others, but use a pencil when it comes to their own personal commitments.**

Leveraging the preceding recommendations, let's revisit and expand on the networking example from earlier in this chapter: "I don't have enough experience or credibility to network with highly successful entrepreneurs."

Most people do not *love* to network. But effective business owners prioritize it like drinking water. To gain experience and competency:

1. Isolate networking as the habit that is holding you back.
2. Go head to head by repeatedly blocking off weekly dates/times to get out and network in a variety of environments. Remember to use a Sharpie, not a pencil!
3. First bump yourself. You are doing something that feels hard, which creates feelings of pride. Acknowledging this perpetuates forward motion and hard things don't stay as hard.
4. Reflect on how to refine the skill. Leverage the momentum you gained from the experience and go tackle the task again with more expertise this time.
5. Reward yourself in proportion to the win. Ziplining with a friend, tickets to Outkast, pedicure? Reinforce the cycle!

The Power of Becoming an Effective Communicator

If you don't have the self-image and confidence to communicate effectively, you won't be heard. Or at least, no one will truly listen. You have to learn how to connect and influence as a side hustler. Communication is your medium. Many try and sidestep growth here because it's uncomfortable and vulnerable and because you've sold yourself a story and you keep buying— or even more dangerous, because you think you are already good at it!

Realize that without the ability to affect other people's behavior or thinking you'll struggle to build a business of significant proportion. On a scale of 1 to 10, how much influence do you have? How does your spirit and affect impact others? Do you emit generous energy? If people can't *feel* your presence or deeper commitment to get to know them or to your cause, then it's hard for people to know you, understand you, or rally behind your mission.

Passion is a huge contributor for getting people's buy in, and it doesn't have to be big and showy. It's often communicated through both verbal and nonverbal cues. Passion isn't a personality type, and neither is success. It's an impactful style of being. When you live your life with extra oomph, you are way more likely to influence others!

Figure out what makes you feel passionate, whether it be the actual work you are doing or the end result the work will create long term, and be emotive about that thing. Let people know how you genuinely feel on a deeper level. It helps people *know* you. That in itself creates meaningful energy and connection. And those are the people you should *want* to find you! Expressing yourself authentically also positions you to better identify your community as discussed in Chapter 3.

> **When you broadcast what you believe in, the right people will find you.**

There are many forms of communication, all of great importance, but we'd like to unpack them individually, as they each have learning points that are specific. And here's the rub: everyone tends to think they are better communicators than they actually are, and there is nothing more dangerous to a business owner than thinking they are a good communicator when they are marginal or weak. In this section, we *need* you to look inward and start working on these skills. Even great communicators will work to become stronger, why should you be an exception?

Recommendations to Grow Your Nonverbal Communication

1. **Appearance.** Look sharp and represent yourself well. You don't need to take a cookie-cutter approach, but be mindful of how your attire, grooming, Zoom lighting, and other aesthetics affect your brand, how you feel and other's perception of you.

2. **Put your phone down and take your headphones off.** Your Beats by Dre are creating a serious buffer between you and humanity. Literally and figuratively. If you're overly disconnected when you are out in the world, it makes it tough to connect. Whether you're on public transportation or in the waiting room at the dentist, put your phone down and take a moment to engage with other human beings and give yourself a shot at adding value to other people. As an example, we have created many business partnerships that have become decade-plus relationships, as a function of being out in the world ready to engage.

3. **Adjust your energy level.** We see a lot of people fail in business by not being able to get on the same frequency as other human beings. If you're naturally lower energy, feel free to take it up several notches (if you're a theater major, please tone it down a solid four or five notches). Don't overlook this point. Most people operate within the standard deviation, but few strike a perfect balance, so you likely need to do some adjusting. It's about more than just *mindfulness*; you might need to *learn to modulate and change.*

Carrie here. In leading a women's book club with a wide range of personality types, we discussed temperaments and acknowledged how it feels when engaging with others who communicate with different levels of energy. Those with laid back personalities felt completely overwhelmed and disconnected when others come on too strong or too energetic. Those with more outgoing natures felt insecure when people show little emotion—as it feels they may not be liked. These are helpful realizations very few people have but can shed invaluable light on how our engagement, or vibe, can break or build connection with others.

4. **Be aware of your body movement and expressions.** Movement that is unnecessary or repetitive in nature is often a sign of

nervousness or lack of confidence. Confidence is represented with poise and deliberate movement. Begin taking stock of quirks or habits you may have such as playing with your hair, extreme eye contact, excessive hand gestures or the opposite—little expression or gestures at all. Another example is having an offputting handshake. Nothing worse than getting the limp noodle or the bone crusher handshake. Be willing to ask a mentor or others you respect about ways you can improve here.

5. **Smile more.** We know, we know, you've heard this one too many times, but have you implemented it? Smiling = warmth. Human beings prefer warm versus cold vibes, period. *Many are racking their brain trying to identify complicated technical changes they should make, or overworking themselves entirely, when simply smiling more and radiating more joy is one of the most impactful changes they can make.*

Tips to Grow Your Verbal Communication

One's ability to effectively deliver a message is what separates instructors from influence-based *leaders*. You can probably think of an authority who delivered content to you over the years that didn't create any real impact. This is much different when you think of a leader who not only *influenced* you but further *empowered* you as their style, tone, message, and approach drew you to make a change. It's valuable to take time to unpack those distinctions—what created that differential in effectiveness?

Our Top Recommendations for Improving Your Verbal Communication Skills

1. **Observe those who use an approach that you appreciate and is successful.** Watch online videos, attend live talks, or listen to podcasts. Who do you connect with? What resonates? Which type of modeling fits who you are and what you are trying to portray? It's probably a hybrid, but you have to figure it out for yourself by studying stellar communicators.

   You also want to pay attention to communicators *you do not like* and understand *why*. Notice how when some people speak, you find it genuinely easy to listen . . . and when others speak, you are so deep into your own thoughts (about why your spouse can't seem to hold themselves back from buying more decorative pillows) that their voice becomes background music to your more interesting thoughts. These are wonderful people to *not duplicate.*

2. **Emulate the approach of those you admire.** Your interactions don't have to be monumentally significant to practice these skills. It's about compounded effort. Frustrating customer service reps make for a great practice space! Be intentional in your practice so these skills and styles can become autonomic and effortless with time. It might feel manual initially, but that's the infancy of most worthwhile change.

3. **Develop awareness of your desire to talk instead of listen.** Listening is a central soft skill. Many people speak relentlessly but ultimately communicate very little because they are not engaging their one-person audience. There's no back and forth. We have all experienced interactions where there is little to no reciprocation and it creates distance versus closeness.

    Don't be the person talking incessantly and not picking up on the verbal or nonverbal "we are done listening" cues from the audience. If you're talking to someone and they are checking their wrist (and don't even have a watch on), let that be a red flag you are being verbose. For the betterment of humanity and your relationships, please watch for verbal, tonal, and physical cues when you are in dialogue with others. *It is generally better to leave people a few minutes before they want you to leave; this leaves people more excited to see you the next time around.* Think of conversations like a volleyball match: you get three touches on the ball and then you have to send it back over to the other side of the net. Bump, set, spike, not bump, bump, bump, bump . . .

    Also, learn when it's appropriate to provide someone with a teaser-trailer or full-feature film. *Typically,* when someone asks you how your day has been, it's *not* an opportunity to tee off extensively on the terrible. Few people want to hear about how hard it was to guzzle down your electrolyte solution pre-colonoscopy. Furthermore, if you are an engineer and someone asks you how your day was at work, no one wants to hear *exactly* what you did.

Unless, of course, you are talking to another engineer. In that case, give it all you got!

The problem with poor communication skills is *rarely will someone directly call you out.* They just stop taking your phone calls, responding to your texts, or inviting you to parties or get-togethers. If you're already particularly unaware, even these social cues get overlooked. You have to pause and assess whether you create a give-and-take environment and ask yourself, "How do I make people *feel* when they are with me?" Do people come back for more, or do they slowly and politely inch away from you, physically and emotionally, like you're carrying something contagious?

Many people might go their entire lives thinking *other* people are just not friendly or that *others* are arrogant. It's more likely they are not taking a genuine interest in others, or being interesting. Everyone has that neighbor they dodge because getting sucked into their orbit is going to be a black hole on your time and energy. Be careful, if you can't think of that person—you might *be them.*

4. **Minimize your nonwords.** Listening to someone say "um," "ahh," or "like" excessively is painful, uninteresting, and certainly not influential. Again, this is often indirectly displaying a lack of confidence or clarity from the person delivering. Everyone has their comfort words. In addition to getting feedback from others, we recommend recording yourself on both video and audio. *Listening to yourself talk (although usually uncomfortable) is one of the best ways to get feedback on how you actually sound.*

5. **Minimize your negative talk tracks.** Some people may enjoy engaging in negative discussion and gossip, but many do not. It's certainly not a great way to increase your influence in a kind way. It's *OK* to share challenges or health issues you have encountered, but to belabor them constantly or get stuck in all the bad things happening to you or in the world can be tiresome for others around you.

6. **Ask thoughtful questions.** People love to talk about themselves, and even more, they love a good listener! Delivering thoughtful questions forges relationships and helps you know how to serve

people better. As a business owner this is beneficial for many reasons; for example, selling a product to a customer is anchored in asking quality questions so you can understand their actual needs.

7. **Actually care.** Carrie here, and I shared this with Craig once and it blew his mind. Craig's response was, "Huh, I've never thought about it *that* way." If you are the type of person who is by nature less empathetic or curious, you may be missing a huge opportunity to connect with people and deepen your influence.

The Power of Public Speaking

Public speaking is a considerably different skill set from other forms of communication. You might be brilliant from an intelligence standpoint or be an incredible strategist, but if you aren't conveying your message effectively as a speaker, it can limit your impact. The same goes for casting a vision to an audience, empowering and unifying an organization, or energizing other human beings—if you can't speak effectively in front of groups, then you better have the time and energy to meet with everyone *individually*.

Even communicating to small groups of people is a form of public speaking. As a side hustler, the more success you have, the larger your audiences will be. As many employees do not get much experience in this arena, they often tighten up and are unprepared, thereby limiting the growth of their side hustle.

So How Do You Improve Your Public-Speaking Skills?

▸ Observe others who are effective specifically at engaging an audience and observe those who are not. What makes each that way? Watch for clear reasons why.

▸ Convey more in less time. Be succinct and *get to the point*. When we are verbose it's not *if* but *when* we will lose our audience. Work to share an hour of content in 20 minutes. People will hang on to your every word.

▸ Develop stronger eye contact (look in the camera lens, not at yourself, and if in person, at your audience).

▸ Execute variation in pitch, tone, volume, and velocity—it keeps the human brain engaged. *Oftentimes, it's not the content that is the issue, it's how we deliver it!*

- ▶ Practice by creating content on social media! It is a brilliant way to sharpen your skills through the written word or video.
- ▶ Have stronger takeaways and calls to action. What can people *implement* from your thought process?
- ▶ Be more *you* . . . when people listen, they're looking for authenticity, not your representative. Open up, and be more vulnerable and transparent about your journey. People love hearing the struggle-*victory* stories not just a struggle-*struggle* story. Too much of this converts to complaining and is not empowering.
- ▶ As you gain comfort, play around with emoting more. This makes your story more compelling and humanizes your conviction. It also makes you more memorable. The more we emote the more others are likely to listen.
- ▶ Get a coach or mentor who can give you real feedback, good and bad!
- ▶ Join an association or club to practice regularly.

Many people make the mistake of believing public speaking is only a talent. But truly, it is a skill, a skill that can be learned. Don't write yourself off as being incapable. Get to work refining this skill; your growth in this arena is like adding a sub-woofer to your messaging.

The Symbiotic Relationship of Leadership and Self-Image

A common denominator of strong leadership is a strong self-image. Luckily, you can grow both simultaneously. We have talked about influence in the context of communication but now let's discuss this in the context of building an organziation, community, or team. John Maxwell describes the idea of the Law of the Lid in his book *21 Irrefutable Laws of Leadership* and writes, "Personal and organizational effectiveness is proportionate to the strength of leadership." He also writes, "Leadership is influence." When you limit your leadership development, you also limit your ability to influence those you work and network with, whereby limiting the impact of your product or service.

We urge you to elevate where you believe you max out on your leadership. Imagine the same you but with significantly more influence—what does that look like, is that something you can incorporate into your future

Life Vision? Even if you are a business of one, it doesn't take a lot of imagination to visualize how impactful growing your leadership can be for your side hustle.

As leadership is a monster topic, we cannot cover the full spectrum here. There are books and *libraries* dedicated to this. But let's explore ways to build on your leadership, specifically through growing your self-image and for the benefit of scaling your side hustle.

1. Build Your Emotional Intelligence

Leadership *requires* an immense amount of emotional durability and maturity. When you're working with people and building organizations, not only do you have to manage your own emotions, but you're often on the receiving end of others. People can be all over the map—intense, irrational, erratic, high, then low, then high again extremists. Leaders who skillfully manage interpersonal relationships and the ups and downs the emotional brain produces are said to have a high emotional quotient (EQ). You can check out the body of work by the researcher who made EQ famous, Daniel Goleman . . . but for purposes of this section, we want you to be aware of developing an EQ to help you form relationships, sense when a conflict is arising, and use compassion to mitigate a misunderstanding.

No matter what your industry, if you're attempting to lead people, you are picking up a dual-sided coin. You experience all the joy and fuzzy feelings, but you also have to toughen the heck up. Carrie here and I can attest to having massive growth in my emotional resiliency over my business career. It's not easy to measure, but when I consider how I would have handled a certain situation at year 1 of business ownership versus year 3 or 10, it's evident how much durability has been built . . . and how it has changed my ability to retain clients, business partners and my overall happiness. Developing a thick skin ultimately enables you to have composure, be less reactive with others, and lean in toward empowerment. It's hard to authentically lead or empower people if you are emotionally charged by their behaviors.

Let's take practical steps to build awareness around Goleman's five distinct categories for building EQ.

1. **Self-Awareness.** List your top three strengths and weaknesses. Also list three ways can you highlight your strengths better as an

entrepreneur. How can you offset or develop around the areas of growth? Be specific and actionable.

2. **Self-Regulation.** STOP. Take seven deep breaths. As you breath, focus on gratitude and being present. How does this shift your overall energy? Attitude? Notice the benefits and use deep breathing as a tool in your toolbelt for stronger self-regulation.

3. **Intrinsic motivation.** Identify three non-external rewards and wins in the day to day that come from being in the pursuit of building your side hustle. As an example, while creating video content on social media, instead of focusing on the likes, hone in on the feeling of growth in your communication skills and development.

4. **Empathy.** Think of a difficult interaction you had recently. Were there emotional undertones you missed? How can you tune into these cues better? Replay this scenario using more empathy. How would things have played out differently?

5. **Social skills.** Pause and send an email or text to someone in your network who has been helpful or influential. This type of praise and genuine edification elevates others and strengthens relationships. How can you make this habit a priority in leading people?

Through incorporating small but valuable exercises like these and building mindfulness around your emotions, you can become better equipped to lead yourself and others. Emotion is a huge piece of the human experience and plays a major role in our relationships and business!

2. Increase Your Adaptability Quotient (AQ)

There are always variables you can't control. The capacity to change or adapt and call audibles when unforeseen challenges arise, is your adaptability quotient (AQ). For us, this has been one of our biggest assets. Even if we are not the smartest or most talented, we've always known we can adapt.

A major challenge of growing a side hustle, having your full-time career, and living a life is they all need to be rocking in tandem. You have to get skilled at managing the many variables and fluctuations. When life is going well, it's easy to stick to habits and goals, but how do you push through when life gets tough? Most people think, "Once I get through *this*, then I'll do *that* and be steady." It's crucial to be able to grow through less than perfect conditions because . . . that's life.

For a business owner it's also critical to factor in economic cycles, competitors, advancements in technology, and so on. When one is willing to course correct, change their product line to match current trends, or pivot strategies altogether they are better able to survive and flourish.

Develop enough perspective so you can take a balcony view of your life and your business and you can effectively reframe challenges and adapt accordingly. As an example, when someone goes through the life milestone of having a newborn baby, their time availability may change. They are in the thick of it and may feel the need to throw in the towel on their side hustle; however, a great way to reframe one's limited time or energy capacity is to step back and figure out where the most important places to invest actually are. Oftentimes, people are overinvesting in certain areas of their business, and when they drill in closer to their vision and values, they can reallocate their resources accordingly. Instead of giving up based on an initially perceived disadvantage, they start working smarter. *People always have time for the most important things if they give themselves a chance to reframe their thinking and adapt.* Many people expend energy wishing for fewer problems when they often just need to be more adaptable in the face of them. In addition, when you think from a space of solutions, your EQ also strengthens, and you can provide so much perspective and stability to those who are looking to you for leadership.

> Grab a pen and paper. Proactively create a list of 2–3 events or challenges that are likely to pop up in the next year as you are building your side hustle. These don't need to be negative situations but areas that could affect your ability to stay consistent with growing your business. List 3 actions you can take to proactively position yourself better for the changes you've identified. This work will allow you to be better prepared emotionally, mentally and strategically. They may still rock your boat but you won't capsize.

3. Identify and Focus on Your Sphere of Influence

It is easy to get caught in the trap of taking out your frustrations on things you can't control, because you haven't taken ownership of the things you actually can. As an example, you can be frustrated about having a low-revenue month, or you can assess your work ethics, skills, or strategy and you'll likely feel a lot more empowered versus disgruntled and discouraged. You can't control the market or individual clients and their decisions, but you can have a big enough sample size and let the numbers work in your favor.

Anchor yourself within your sphere of influence. Your thoughts, attitude, and work ethic are valuable places to start. *It takes the same amount of energy to complain about the negative as it does to get working on resolutions.* Leaders get good at converting the negative energy into solutions.

Ownership Exercise

Step 1: Think of a scenario that didn't go well in your adult life.

Step 2: Recall features and details of this experience without taking any responsibility. Place blame on all other parties or circumstances involved but yourself.

Step 3: Replay the entire scenario but take full ownership. What role did you play? What could you have done differently? Prepared better? Responded more effectively to?

Step 4: Meditate on which version of your story feels more empowering. Welcome to business *owner*ship!

---

4. Be Honest with Yourself and Transparent with Others

The best leaders know they have changes to make and view it as opportunity. Being honest about your strengths and weaknesses, and having a willingness to grow, is the sign of a secure leader. You can be your own biggest challenge on the journey. Learning how to make the necessary internal changes can be the most inspiring attribute to others you are leading. *One of our favorite things to observe is watching mentors or leaders we know continue to evolve.* This increases our respect for these leaders. The question is, are you this kind of leader? When is the last time a team member you lead was impressed by your willingness to level up?

The more you grow your self-image and hold positions of leadership, the bolder and more candid you become in sharing your perspective, insights, and opinions. When in a leadership role, it is a responsibility to speak the truth or institute "radical transparency," as Ray Dalio calls it. While most of us lack the self-image to speak our minds candidly, strong leaders are highly skilled at this, especially when it comes to challenges, personality conflicts, or competencies. For example, we used to be hesitant to give feedback to the people we led. Now we are more straightforward, but not with the intention of being rude or "right." It is to be helpful and because we have strong enough confidence in our own leadership and communication skills when delivering tough messages.

> **To tell someone a difficult truth is both a privilege and a responsibility of leadership. We believe the world would be a better place and relationships would be more genuine if we all had more courage to be *thoughtfully transparent*.**

Warning: *Don't Get Lost in the Abyss of Personal Development*

Enjoy your personal development journey, but don't get so caught up in the *bliss* that you fall victim to never actually growing your enterprise. There is a trap of becoming addicted to academic epiphanies and feel-good YouTube videos. While a helpful part of the equation, they are only a portion and do not actively grow your side hustle.

We divide business activities into two buckets: *preparation or productivity*. Many are too busy singing from the mountaintops about their personal development (aka preparation). It's not *the worst* problem to have because at the end of the day, at least you're becoming a beautifully evolved person. Be real with yourself and what you're looking to create. Figure out how much time should be invested into preparation and how much should be safeguarded for physically getting out there and being productive. As a leader you need to execute both *simultaneously*.

So as crucial as we believe your self-image and self-development are, and we have invested the first half of this book assembling a foundation, it's time to *get productive*. Our next chapter, discussing common pitfalls, gets you activating immediately while develeoping awareness of the most common missteps along the way.

CHAPTER 7

Common Pain Points on the Journey

Challenges are gifts that force us to search
for a new center of gravity. Don't fight
them. Just find a new way to stand.
—Oprah

We wish a chapter on pain points wasn't necessary and that you didn't have to stumble in your side hustle journey—but that's not realistic. So instead, we want to share some of the most common hurdles business owners experience (ourselves included). By knowing what the most common challenges are, you're more likely to identify them when they arise and either sidestep them entirely or at least preemptively minimize their impact.

Top 11 Pain Points

- Ineffective time and task management
- Reverting back to employee mindset

- ▶ Mistaking revenue for profit
- ▶ Underinvesting, period
- ▶ Serial side hustle hopping and always looking for the new, shiny venture
- ▶ Hiding behind the easy work versus doing the hard work
- ▶ Not being green, malleable, or innovative in your own head or industry
- ▶ Overpricing yourself too early *and* not raising prices later
- ▶ Neglecting personal relationships
- ▶ Not setting clear boundaries
- ▶ Getting caught in the comparison trap

1. Ineffective Time and Task Management

Most side hustlers are woefully underprepared for the craziness that ensues when you really get into the thick of hammering your side business *and* your career. Not to mention other priorities you may have in life. As a result, we see people get steamrolled, unable to compartmentalize their time well, resulting in challenges in either their career, relationships, or simply failing to get their side hustle to a desired level.

Most traditional time-management strategies center on efficiency, which is absolutely important, but if you don't prioritize your activities by aligning them with your values, you can be efficiently doing the *wrong thing*. You end up with a perfectly made bed, washed, ironed, and pressed every morning with mint-crisp dog-eared corners, but zero sales leads for the day. This, of course, is a problem, unless you value perfect tidiness over generating new sales leads. We certainly do not.

Many books stress that people can't really manage time, but instead can manage only their *priorities*. We agree and have been using elements of Stephen Covey's calendar for the last 10 years and also recommend his book *First Things First*.

Covey's philosophy recommends prioritizing your schedule around the week. Why? Because it's easier to navigate your priorities within different roles on a weekly basis. A lot of people don't go to church, call their mother, or work out *every* day, but they certainly can do these things weekly or multiple times in a week.

We became clear about our weekly priorities and how they aligned with our deeper values and vision early on. For us there have been times (OK, almost always) when having the cleanest, most organized home would come at the cost and detriment of chasing our business goals. We had to have quality discussions on housekeeping and chores; otherwise, it was easy to be frustrated by the ongoing pile of clothes in the corner of our bedroom. Make sure you are aware of how your values play out in real life. If you say you value adventure, you need to anticipate and accept you need to be doing adventurous activity on a regular basis, which may come at the expense of lower-valued activities.

To make things even harder when managing our time, our society provides more inputs and stimulus than the human brain was evolutionary designed to handle. Thirty years ago, we did not have Twitter, Netflix, or a phone that is glued to us at all hours of the day. Today an enhanced amount of self-discipline is needed to curb our own impulses. Learn to create accountability systems—people *need* accountability more than they want it. Things that have helped us include creating the right associations, accountability partners, a disciplined calendar, touch points with our mentors, and short- and long-term rewards.

When it comes to managing activities and efficiency specifically, it's important to determine what is both necessary to get done and what only you can do! Many business owners see their business as an extension of who they are, and many aren't able to scale or automate effectively because they cannot legitimately identify and empower someone who can eventually duplicate their efforts. They are a one-man or one-woman show and take a lot of pride in being unduplicatable, the hero. But ultimately if you want to build a sandcastle and at some point take your hands out of it and *not* have it fall apart, then developing a strategy for scaling out of certain tasks or roles is crucial. We have fallen in this trap many times by being too control-oriented versus influence driven or succession-planning focused.

You can always start small when it comes to delegation. Oftentimes, people go from one extreme or the other, but finding a middle ground and building up can be more practical. Hiring people to do work *you* don't need to do can buy you back so much of your time! You can then go do what no one else can do for your business *or* just go enjoy other aspects of your life.

Here's a funnel of questions to help you both prioritize and become more efficient when it comes to daily tasks:

1. Is this task or activity important to me, my side hustle, or my values? If not, can I kindly decline or *just not do it?*

2. If it needs to be done, can I *automate* the task or work in some way?
3. If not, can I *delegate* this task?
4. If not, how and when can I complete this task in the most efficient time? What is the deadline?
5. As I continue to perform this task, can I eventually drop, automate, or delegate this in the future? There are many tasks we cannot delegate now, but strong leaders build others and empower those around them to gain the skill to replace them so they can elevate.

Whatever you can systematize makes your life easier and creates fewer moving parts. Even simple things such as autopayments or automated ordering profiles for consumable goods can clear up space on your ongoing to-do list.

> We were blessed with mentors who helped us assess our finances and recommended we delegate activities we are not good at—*and* do not enjoy. We now employ a cleaning company, bug company, home security service, lawn care service, weed service, irrigation service, a live-in nanny, and at one point, a *professional organizer*. It wouldn't have made sense for us to delegate these tasks when we were 22 years old—our market value wasn't strong enough and we didn't have the money. But as we created more success, some of these delegations have become nonnegotiable for scaling up.

2. Reverting Back to Employee Mindset

Having an employee mindset is not a bad thing, but having an employee mindset when you are growing a business can be detrimental. With entrepreneurship being strongly accessible, side hustlers often start businesses but fall short in adopting a hardcore ownership mentality. Since most side hustlers are also still employees, it's common to default to the employee scripting. A handful of the biggest shifts a business owner has to work hard to make are:

▶ **Predictablity and Stability vs. Variability.** When you work for two weeks and get paid for two weeks, it's predictable. You have your salary, benefits, and usually a set schedule. As an entrepreneur you may work your guts out, have an unpredicitable schedule for years, and be underpaid—learn to embrace that as an entrpreneur there are seasons for sowing and reaping.

▶ **Being the Smartest vs. Finding Those Smarter.** Employees typically aspire to be the smartest person in the room, or see those smarter as their competition. This can be a major source of pride, but when you own your own business surrounding yourself with those smarter than you becomes an asset!

▶ **Being Parented vs. Self-Parenting.** No one is coming to save you as a business owner. You have to be willing to show up and create the work, without much to show for it right away—and sometimes with a lot of criticism. Elon Musk recently responded to a question about what words of encouragement he would give an entrepreneur. He replied, "If you need words of encouragement don't become an entrepreneur." You have to move past needing hand holding, a syllabus, someone micromanaging you, and getting your diapers changed.

▶ **Focusing on Fear vs. Vision.** Many employees stay employees because they fear the unknown, or because all the things that could go wrong is greater than their willingness to chase the opportunity or vision they may have. Bringing this default setting to the entrepreneurial world can be catastrophic. This doesn't mean you don't have fears, you just have to be willing to mitigate them as you move forward despite the chance of failure. The vision is more important.

3. Mistaking Revenue for Profit

A lot of budding and even experienced entrepreneurs make the mistake of focusing exclusively on revenue when the real goal should be profit. Of course, revenue must come first, but it is nearsighted to not be thinking about how to make *and keep* some of the money.

We know several people who have attempted to start an online coaching business. The mindset was this: find 20 clients, charge each client $5,000 per year, and make $100,000 in *profit*! No problem, right? Wrong.

How will you find these clients? Will you have a website, and if so, how will you maintain it? Will you have marketing, branding, travel, or other costs to account for? Will you be a part of a networking group with annual fees? Will you get certified? Who will handle your accounting, bookkeeping, and legal contracts? What if a customer doesn't pay you? The list goes on and on. It is clear that $100,000 is not what you end up keeping.

The point is this: too many people start side hustles thinking that the sales they make are essentially the same as their profit—it's a classic employee way of thinking about income generation. Don't mess this up. On top of a budget, make sure to run strong projections prior to going into business and on an annual basis.

It is also important to understand that when you do create "enough" revenue, you don't necessarily *have* to reinvest all your profits to generate more sales. You now have options. Rather than spending all your efforts growing your top-line revenue, you can consider becoming more profitable at the same level of revenue by finding ways to increase your automation or outsource a lot of the work to buy back time.

For example, let's say you start a side hustle in the landscaping industry. Over the next 10 years you eventually grow it to a full-fledged business generating $600,000 in revenue, with $130,000 in net profit (assuming you don't take a salary). You could then take a year or two to sharpen your systems, secure your client base, get lean by paying off any debt, and transfer your skills and the management to a couple of employees. Eventually, you can promote your key understudy to actively run your business at $60,000 per year and keep $70,000 per year for yourself (*while doing minimal work*). If you have a humble personal budget and manage your finances well, you might be able to live off less than $70,000 per year. Over time, you build up some savings, diversify, start or invest in another business, and chase whatever else your heart desires. In addition, at some point you could choose to cash out and sell the business or assets, likely worth at least a few hundred thousand dollars.

Or you can do what most small business owners do: acquire more clients to generate more revenue, borrow money to buy more equipment, hire more employees, and increase your overhead, risk—and likely stress. Then spend that extra money on a bigger home, a boat, and more cars, and take the next 30 years of your life working super hard because you need to keep your revenue high to cover all your business and personal expenses.

This is why we have spent so much time helping you develop your Life Vision and what you value. Yes, you need a certain amount of top-line revenue to achieve success, but depending on what you want in life, you can reverse engineer your business from the onset for the revenue and profit levels you need to create the life you want.

4. Underinvesting, Period

When we first began growing our side hustles, we were frugal in terms of our personal expenses but at the same time completely willing to make any necessary investments to make sure our business babies grew. We have been on the same page in this regard and share similar mindsets. Discerning what are helpful, nonnegotiable investments to make can be difficult as a new entrepreneur, which is why coaching, mentorship, and educating yourself is crucial. It's important to feel good and feel confident about where you are allocating your resources, since they are finite. With an employee background, you will likely have to fight a natural tendency to hold back or shortcut certain investments.

When considering investing into your business, here's a short funnel you can use as a tool in discern where to put your money:

1. What is the specific function of this investment? Is that function critical?
2. Will this investment help me solve an urgent or important problem in my business?
3. If I have the funds, do I know for sure this investment will pay off, at least in the mid- to long-term?
4. Can I go without this purchase?
5. Is there something better to invest my money or time into right now?
6. Will this purchase let me automate or delegate a task and save me time I can better invest elsewhere?
7. Will this purchase help me generate more revenue?

5. Serial Side Hustle Hopping and Always Looking for the New, Shiny Venture

We have unfortunately met many aspiring entrepreneurs who are *eternally* aspiring. One of their primary challenges is they are perpetually onto the next new thing when their current project gets hard or *is no longer shiny*. No doubt, every business gets to a space that is mundane or repetitive. While the grass may be greener on the other side, it is often because someone else has done all the mundane work already; you are just seeing the finished product.

It is impossible to build anything of substance if every six months or year you leave one side hustle to start another. If you find yourself in this pattern, *stop* immediately. There is nothing wrong with taking a step back and asking yourself questions, such as, *Is this business still viable? Did some other unforeseen macro-economic situation radically change my scenario? Is my business damaging my marriage or other important relationships or aspects of my Life Vision?*

However, if you see yourself developing a pattern of business hopping, do yourself a giant favor—get a mentor and start associating with live entrepreneurs who have built real businesses. If you lay out your story for them, they can provide you rumble strips. You may need them.

6. Hiding Behind the Easy Work Versus Doing the Hard Work

When you start a business, it's easy to get caught up in the romanticized bliss of handing out your very own business cards, designing your logo or website, and looking the part. Don't get us wrong: many aspects of front-end work are important, but sometimes they are too fun, especially compared to facing yourself in the mirror and having to make interpersonal changes, going out into the jungle, hustling, and getting beat up with rejection.

The most effective activities are usually the hardest and least desirable, but they tend to fix most of the challenges of running your own business when you go out and do them. Creating sales is a great example of this. *If you created another few million in revenue from your side hustle, would you be able to solve most of the other business challenges?* Couldn't you hire, outsource, delegate, or straight up sell the side hustle and cash out if your sales are strong enough? We understand making actual sales is not always the most glamorous work. And we feel you—top-line revenue doesn't solve *all* your problems; that's why we have other topics in this book. Clearly some attention needs to be paid to important items like accounting or continuing to develop your actual product, but don't let all the other busy work and administrative tasks be at the detriment to revenue-generating activities. Create enough revenue and you can always hire people to run your business for you.

If you are not the type of person who enjoys adding top-line revenue to your business, either get over it and develop the learning mindset we have been talking about, or partner or hire someone who does. Too much emphasis on color-coding your file drawer at the expense of your total sales is about as useful as trying to mop the floor peak hours at a college house party.

7. Not Being Green, Malleable, or Innovative in Your Own Head or Industry

One of the best parts about entrepreneurship is *the learning curve never ends.* One of the hardest parts is the learning curve never ends. Roles change, the economy changes, you change, the world changes. In life, change is the one guarantee. Learn to embrace change instead of raging against it. Harness the adventure of being on the cutting edge of innovation. Our business landscape looks different today than it did 14 years ago—do you think your environment will go unchanged over the next 14 years?

As an example, we weren't writers until we wrote this book. Every part of this process has been new (and we didn't have to write it, we chose to). We aren't saying the learning has been easy or always fun; in fact, at times it's been *painfully* grueling—yet worth it. When you stay green and in a learning mode, something exciting and challenging is always happening. Innovating and learning keep the boredom away.

8. *Overpricing* Yourself Initially or *Not Raising Prices* Once You Have Established Your Brand and Grown Your Value

Hear this loud and clear: there is nothing wrong with charging premium pricing for a premium service! If you are the Bentley of your industry, go for it! But not only do you need to *be it*, your potential customer also needs to *believe it*. If you don't have a reputation, strong brand, or robust portfolio with a track record for success, you may want to kick off more humbly. All the more reason to use a *side* hustle because you won't have the same level of pressure to generate revenue, let alone big revenue early on.

We give some more specific examples of undercharging for services in Chapter 10 about raising capital. Keep in mind though: once you are successful, customers will also pay for perceived value, and oftentimes if something has low cost, people may value it less. Once you have strong branding and a clear value that you have delivered to many customers, develop the confidence to charge accordingly.

Don't be afraid to revisit your pricing structures regularly. With basic inflation and an ever-changing and dynamic economy, you should be dynamic in your pricing as well.

9. Neglecting Personal Relationships

Our closest relationships can create a ton of resistance, and make growing a side hustle extremely difficult if we are not being thoughtful and mindful about how we navigate them. Since you're leveraging your evenings and weekends to build your side hustle, and that is often important time with one's significant other, this is a key pitfall to be aware of. Trying to separate a business owner from their business is emotional. You created it, grew it, and gave birth to it. There is a lot of attachment. As a result, your closest person might not understand this if they have never owned a business and it's cramping your quality time with them.

Although your side adventure has potential to place additional strain on your closest relationships, it doesn't have to if you are:

▸ **Candid about what you're doing** so your loved one can understand why you are making the investments you are. Can they
  explain what you are working on? If they can't, then you are missing out on a point of connection and leverage from potentially one
  of your best brand ambassadors and cheerleaders!
▸ **Clear on your schedule** so there are no unnecessary withdrawals,
  unkept promises, or lack of accountability.
▸ **Synergistic** with your partner, so they can be a part of your journey,
  or at least a supporter of it. Even small synergies can be a big win! If
  they are up for it, give them a role. Maybe it's something as simple as helping you brainstorm your social media content strategy,
  helping you with video or branding, or handling the bookkeeping
  or accounting. Play to their strengths. This synergy is unifying as
  it gives them a window of insight into what the heck you do. Even
  if it is only 1 or 2 percent of the work—if they feel some sense of
  ownership and involvement, they are more likely to understand you
  better as you go through challenges or celebrate in the victories!

▸ *Not* **pushing too hard** for their involvement, or more than they are willing to contribute. Having your spouse bitterly processing invoices on a Saturday afternoon when he or she would like to be out kayaking is a sure way to create emotional withdrawals.

▸ **Constructing your 10-year Vision together** so everyone's long-term goals are identified, and deeper needs get met. When there are two parties involved, both parties matter. Just because you run a business doesn't mean you take priority in all aspects of existence. Tend to your partnership and get on the same page. Oftentimes, slowing down to connect and align can help you speed up long term and lead a happier life. You can discuss how your goals for your business can fit snugly into and be a contributing part of the 10-year Vision, true to the foundation of this book.

Entrepreneurship is already challenging enough, so don't create extra hurdles for your business or sacrifice those most important to you. Remember, the quality of your life is heavily influenced by the quality of your relationships.

10. Not Setting Clear Boundaries

You knew it was coming . . . here it is. The B word. We talked about how important it is to maintain healthy personal relationships. On the flip side, we see many people neglect their own Life Vision in the name of catering to everybody else's. If you really want to run through the finish line of your own personal goals, then you have to figure out the right balance of remaining generous and attentive toward others while keeping your own priorities sacred. When you don't set effective boundaries, not only do your relationships suffer but so does your personal livelihood. The book *Boundaries: When to Say Yes, How to Say No to Take Control of Your Life* by Dr. Henry Cloud and Dr. John Townsend does a remarkable job highlighting the ways people undercut their boundaries in the name of being loving.

> **Setting and protecting your boundaries without apologies will make you more aerodynamic as an entrepreneur *and* a better steward of healthy relationships. There is so much power in a graceful No!**

11. Getting Caught in the Comparison Trap

No matter what Life Phase you are in, successful business owners are a unique species, oftentimes a little weird, and almost always fanatical. Comparing any two paths is like dropping a Van Gogh into a modern art museum and expecting it to make sense. It shouldn't. And for the record, we love Van Gogh *and* modern art.

While our peers were having quintessential camping weekends, enjoying Tuesday night softball league, buying nice homes or fancy cars, there were years we were flying around the country, changing dirty diapers in hotel rooms with a screaming toddler in tow, all while running back-to-back weekend appointments in coffee shops without any guarantee of a return on investment. You'll have your own stories that may or may not resemble ours, but the bottom line is relatability might go out the window when you are actively pursuing a nontraditional lifestyle. Don't compare notes unless you do so with a mentor, but if you do, use those notes purely for entertainment between friends versus as a benchmark on whether you're doing it "right." Luckily, there are plenty of ways to hedge against comparison and put yourself in a healthy, helpful headspace.

Shut down social media feeds that don't help your pursuit or focus. You always have the option to completely disconnect from individuals who irk you, especially when you find their negative or distracting influence lingering in your life for longer than what's helpful. Interesting note, many successful people on social media have significantly more people following them than they follow. Why? They are busy building, doing, and influencing.

Recognize when you're being downright irrational. People tend to compare their weaknesses to others' strengths and it doesn't do them any favors. As a side hustler, it's common to start stacking up the tough parts of business ownership against the perks and simplicity of exclusively being an employee. An example would be getting upset that your buddies have few responsibilities after work hours, and in your frustration not acknowledging the fact that you are diversifying, growing your skill sets, and likely leveling up as a person. It's a classic scenario of putting your life under a microscope when times are challenging and looking at someone else's setup with a telescope.

Be patient with your emotions. You will have your moments or days when you question what the heck you're doing. Honor those feelings. They are likely fleeting, and you can move through them as they pass versus anchoring yourself in them and ultimately amplifying them.

— — —

Even though we debrief you on common pitfalls in a book, it does not mean you won't face them on your journey. But our hope is that this gives you a framework and prepares you better for how to get through hurdles more agilely. Of course, if you can avoid them altogether, more power to you. We take a deeper look at one of the root challenges that drives many of these pain points in our next chapter as we examine a very important side hustling skill in which most people are never trained: decision making.

CHAPTER 8

Decision Making and Executing Like a CEO

*Truly successful decision making relies
on a balance between deliberate
and instinctive thinking.*
—Malcolm Gladwell

Business owners are required to make decisions *incessantly*. On a daily and even hourly basis, side hustlers face decisions on everything from marketing campaigns, websites, social media, inventory management, referral programs, and outsourcing; the decisions never stop. Employees have decisions to make as well, but they tend to be narrower in scope and often have protocol and guardrails in place (although often more sophisticated in higher levels of management). The number of decisions a business owner needs to execute can be a rude awakening for many side hustlers, who are often unprepared.

Business owners get paid to solve problems, and as business coaches we have witnessed *strong patterns* in those who are poor and those who are skilled in their problem-solving and decision-making ability. Although not synonymous, solving problems and making decisions do go hand in hand. They both require critical thinking skills, and many decisions need to be made on the journey of solving a problem—and there are plenty to tend to. It's part of the gig and requires being swift on one's feet and solution oriented. These are nonnegotiable skill sets as you work to thrive through the mess of dissatisfied customers, delayed raw material, unpaid customer invoices, and damaged products.

We have seen many engineers, accountants, doctors, and other intelligent and highly trained individuals, to put it frankly, *suck* at being entrepreneurs. While folks in these categories pride themselves on being "smart" (and they often are), that quality in and of itself does not make you a successful business owner. You can be a proficient problem solver and still lack effective decision-making skills in a business environment that get you closer to where you want to be—and with fruitful outcomes. When you start a *solopreneur adventure*, simply being intelligent is *not enough to win.*

As an example, Craig once had a small business owner send him a spreadsheet analyzing a new company vehicle purchase. The difference between the owner's options for the truck he was purchasing was only about $20,000, yet the owner had invested hours into his spreadsheet. Not to mention he had sent it to his CPA and banker and wanted their pros and cons. Weeks later the business owner stopped into the bank and wanted to discuss the issue with Craig again. Craig advised him that all the time he invested *thinking* about the truck should have gone into adding a couple more customers, which would have paid for the difference in cost. As a result of his indecision, the owner was actually *losing* customers because shipments on orders were being delayed.

Opportunity cost as a result of indecision is not always this painfully obvious, but a strong standstill in daily operations and mental momentum can happen when one is hovering over a decision for too long and with too much emotional and mental energy. It is an immense drain and tends to be habitual if a deeper confidence, stronger mindset, and better executive decision-making skills have not been developed.

On the flip side, many aspiring business owners are not analytical enough, making quick and hasty decisions without properly understanding critical data points, and not questioning or thoroughly exploring the repercussions or costs of those decisions.

There is a balance, and properly managing this balance is an important distinction between business owners who flounder and those who flourish. Most people have a propensity to lean toward one extreme or the other. This chapter provides practical tips we have seen help people on how to become more effective in your decision making, so you can execute like a CEO. But while discussing solutions, it's important to understand why it may take too long to make decisions or what may be causing poor decisions altogether.

Frankly we don't have the power to grant you expert decision-making capacity. There's no magic wand. It's your job to figure it out. However, there are *reasons* people struggle. Your best shot at improving is to identify the root pain points that are obstructing your ability to deliberate or they will continue to weigh you down, no matter what tactics you deploy on a surface level. So let's make sure we identify some of these root causes now.

Root Causes of Indecision and Corresponding Solutions

Lack of Confidence

As discussed in Chapter 6, your business will not exceed your self-image. If you lack the inner confidence or self-trust to make decisions quickly and on a consistent basis, you can get caught in a downward spiral. Deferring decisions simply because you don't have the confidence to make them doesn't resolve the issues; in fact, it generally exacerbates them.

Take Action

Would you be better off and have a greater chance of success by making five different attempts than thinking for a week and trying only one—or not trying at *all*? Oftentimes, the business owner taking heaping amounts of action can be in their third time at bat and get a base hit, while the indecisive owner is still trying to theorize how to execute the perfect swing. You don't need to have the confidence you will get it right your first time at bat; you need to have the belief you can get it right *eventually*. As long as the stakes are not extremely high, most of your decisions are not pass/fail.

Surround Yourself with People Who Are Skilled at Taking Action

At times these almost reckless-seeming individuals will blow your mind with how quickly they *just decide* and go do things. You may at times witness mistakes they may make, but also notice that they rarely suffer *fatal consequences* from taking those actions. They also *learn* and they can adjust and do it again! If you have forgotten the value of who you surround yourself with, please revisit Chapter 3, "Finding Your WHO." If you are constantly struggling with indecision, it should come as no surprise that learning from excellent decision makers is one of our top recommendations. Skilled decision makers instill confidence in those around them, and oftentimes provide a refreshing clarity to an otherwise troublesome or heavy situation.

Tiptoeing Around Risk

You can't control everything! Walking across the street is a risk. Eating meat is a risk. Not eating meat can be a risk. The reality is you cannot *eliminate* risk; you can only *manage* to it. At some point you have to let go and stop trying to pretend you can control everything in life, let alone every outcome as an entrepreneur.

Solution: Determine What Is the Worst Case Scenario?

Other than opportunity cost, what are your *real* risks if you take action? If a decision could result in death, bankruptcy, or imprisonment, maybe you should chill and take some time on it. But if it's more like "should you paint the accent wall in your home office in the *Bavarian crème* or the *frosted lemon*," just pick one and *move on*.

> Know that making firm decisions does not mean you won't ever make the wrong one or take on risk. You likely will, and embracing that possibility is one of the many responsibilities that comes with business ownership.

You might also hem and haw and spend countless hours strategizing, making spreadsheets, polling your social media community, and having sleepless nights and *still* make a less than optimal decision. Nothing is completely fail proof, so ask yourself, *Which method of decision making gives me greater happiness and peace?*

Lack of Knowledge

As a new business owner you will come across topics with which you are unfamiliar. If you don't know anything about buying Facebook or Instagram advertising or purchasing software, making decisions may take longer and be more stressful.

Learn a New Skill or Expertise

Sometimes you just need to bite the bullet and invest time into a particular subject. This is especially important when some aspect of your side hustle is going to be continual and you can't outsource it.

Planning to build out a podcast, but you have never conducted a formal interview? Study up. Starting a new bookkeeping side hustle, but you loath selling or finding new customers? It might be time to dive in and develop some sales aptitude. You have to embrace getting outside of the comfort zone; otherwise, you will continually be defined by your current suite of skills. As discussed in Chapter 6, when people learn new skills or develop an expertise their confidence and their decision-making capacity in that arena skyrockets. Besides, do you really believe the skills you have are sufficient to grow a massive profitable side hustle if you never have before?

Carrie here. When jumping on LinkedIn I had very little social media experience. I was one part intimidated and one part excited about the uphill learning curve. I had to work to embrace the newness and the awkward Bambi phase as I was still getting my legs and making sense of it all. I rallied myself around the whole process and made it into an adventure, versus spending a painful amount of time just thinking about it. Learn how to be your own best hype-person and energize yourself around the work.

Overwhelmed by Too Much Information

Have you ever gone into the local hardware store to buy something relatively simple, but then invested too much time determining which flooring, lighting, lamp, or hammer to purchase? When we were building our office, we had hundreds of flooring options, all cross referenced by different pricing, warranties, and quality. At one point, Craig executed a coin flip so we could move on with our lives.

Know When to Stop Seeking Out More Information

In the twenty-first century, people have access to an unlimited amount of info and even more opinions—often masked as fact. Making informed decisions is important, but you can also get lost in stacks of data that can derail you from more important action. You want to focus your energy on things with genuine impact. Learn when to pump the brakes on excessive facts, figures, and options—*not all decisions should be weighted equally and do not all require the same time investment.*

Trust Your Gut

Realize your intuition is a brilliant and powerful force, and when it speaks, you should listen. When people ask us for our opinion on a deeply personal decision or a decision that could go many different directions, we often respond by asking, "What is your gut telling you?" Simple? Yes. Effective? Also, yes.

As you gain more experience, your intuition also deepens. It's both an evolution and a muscle that can be strengthened with enough practice.

You Enjoy Analyzing or Brainstorming Too Much

Many analytic or creative people enjoy the process of running through different scenarios and options. If you are nerdy like Craig and want to invest time doing so for sport and fun, go for it. Just don't pretend you are building your business when the time spent is unnecessary. For the creatives, the Bavarian crème will do just fine for your accent wall.

Ask Yourself, What Is the Opportunity Cost of My Time by Investing More of My Life Thinking About This?

What else could you be working on that may be a better use of your time? Are there other responsibilities that are a greater priority? This requires discipline, to pull yourself out of the rabbit hole in the moment and be honest about what matters. Business owners have to get good at zooming in and zooming out. Why are you making the decision that is in front of you? What is the goal of this decision, and how can it tie back to your larger business goals and Life Vision?

Taking on Too Many Decisions

Are you simply making too many decisions and unwilling to delegate? Choosing how to prioritize your decisions, which decision you should be making and/or which to outsource is where many business owners struggle.

Relinquish Some Control

The notion that someone else may be able to handle work or a decision at 80 or 90 percent your effectiveness, or perhaps even more effectively, is something we had to learn to embrace. Now, who, when, and how much of these decisions you relinquish are important details, but that doesn't mean you can't develop enough trust with others to get there.

If you are unwilling to let go of control, you are likely not accurately considering the best-case possibilities but anchoring yourself emotionally in the worst. Note the worst is always a possibility, but if you put good thought into your partnerships and who you outsource tasks to, as we will discuss in Chapter 9 on your inner circle, you will likely create some massive wins and remove important duties from your plate.

Your Goals Are Superficial

A lot of the things people want and put time or energy into aren't actually what they want. As a result, they are unmotivated to make the decisions necessary to be successful.

Revisit Your WHY(s) and Life Vision

Maybe it's a client you're half-heartedly chasing, a new skill set you are lukewarm about, or a chronically wimpy work ethic. There's a strong possibility you honestly don't care that much about the goal. Your track record and enthusiasm can give you important intel on your earnestness. One's lack of action and strong decision making can be an indication you may just enjoy the idea of it!

Have you ever observed a friend struggling to commit long term in their relationship? Your friend was grappling to understand their indecision but from your outside perspective it was clear they just weren't that into them and as a result were unwilling to commit to the "goal."

Having clarity sets people up to genuinely win in what they focus on. Even though our first businessess were side hustles we treated them like traditional startups we had dropped our life savings into. Because we had clarity on our Life Vision, tough decisions became easier to make and commit to.

Second-Guessing Yourself *After* Making a Decision

If you consistently fall into the trap of questioning and fretting over a decision you already made, then you are likely wasting energy that could be invested elsewhere. In a culture where having access to so many choices is highly valued, many actually struggle to stay confident in the aftermath of making a decision.

Don't Look Back

When you finally make a decisive move forward, give your decision a chance to take flight. If you are anchored in your values, don't worry about the opportunity cost of everything else you said no to by making a decision. Focusing on those other paths, girlfriends, cereal brands (we can all relate to that overwhelming feeling of too many options in the cereal aisle) you didn't choose is self-destructive to the path you *did choose*! It's like dating someone new but continuously stalking your ex on social media. Does this help your current relationship? Or your mental health? When you don't look back, you also give yourself peace of mind. Press pause on the game of mental ping-pong and mitigate post-decision-making fatigue in your life.

> **Realize, a business owner being habitually indecisive leads to *inaction*. Inaction is like kryptonite to an entrepreneur.**

Root Causes of Hasty Decision Making and Corresponding Solutions

Being indecisive can be a wet blanket on your momentum, but the other extreme, being too quick to make decisions, can also have negative repercussions, such as running the ball down the field quickly and confidently—but in the wrong direction. Let's take a look at common reasons for hasty decision making and some corresponding solutions.

Lacking Attention to Detail

Ever hopped into your car and headed out to grab your Thai takeout and realized the restaurant was in Eagle River *Alaska*, not Wisconsin? This happened to us *last week*. Or perhaps you purchased several thousand dollars of inventory only to realize it was measured by meters and not yards? Forgot to figure sales tax into your latest cost calculations? These are cute challenges when reading a book about others' follies, but painful when work has to be redone or profitability has been lost in your own business.

Discerning Which Scenarios Require Big-Picture Execution Versus a Fine-Tooth Comb

When the stakes are high, either slow down and grind out the details, double-check your work, or have someone else do so. It is also important to know which decisions do require more detail or complex thinking and make these decisions at your peak operating times during the day. Doing complex accounting late at night may well be in your wheelhouse. If not, budget a more optimal time so it's not as taxing mentally.

Impatience

Good things come to those who wait? Only sometimes. But for those making decisions like a "bull in a china shop" or with a "get 'er done" mentality, there can be detrimental consequences.

Learn How to Ask the Right Scenario-Based Questions

Noticing patterns of making careless decisions can take time, because you generally need to see the repercussion of the decision to know it was the wrong one. However, the best solution to offset impatience is to start asking quality questions: *What is the source of my impatience? Why am I consistently impatient around this type of decision?* If you confirm a task does deserve your time, ask, *How have I made mistakes on these types of decisions before? What safeguards can I put in place to avoid these again?*

For example, if you are too quick to make promises to customers that you can't deliver on later, take a deep breath and ask yourself, *Can we truly do this in the time frame I am promising?* Or, if you notice yourself chronically running late to appointments, ask yourself, *How can I be more realistic about my timeframes and execution?*

Avoidance or Lack of Interest of Specific Tasks

Have some things that just aren't interesting to you? Don't feel like confirming with your CPA if an expense is tax deductible or not and assume it is, only to pay dearly when tax time comes?

Delegate, Outsource or Automate!

As you execute, know when to loop in an expert or specialist. Decision making and execution don't have to be a solo job. Here is a line of questions for discerning if you need to pull in additional help or perspective: Do you have a partner, staff, or professional expert you can trust to delegate this to? If not and this is a regular decision that needs to be made, can you begin moving in a direction so that six months or two years from now you have empowered someone else to give you air coverage? Who could you train to handle this going forward?

> **Carrie here.** I can remember early on being frustrated by the amount of fine points I had to attend to in regard to budgeting for my business. I converted that annoyance into a motivator to build my business to a certain point so I didn't have to deal with it at all and could completely hand it over to someone else who genuinely loved that task . . . luckily I married a man obsessed with budgeting! Let your distaste become a motivator for growth!

One of the best decisions we made was to outsource our payroll processing. For us, payroll is cumbersome, time consuming, and unenjoyable. Paying a company a few thousand dollars a year to run payroll freed us up to work on more critical components of our businesses.

Also note there are a lot of aspects of entrepreneurship that are insanely boring and mundane. At times you have to flat out get over it. Being willing to power through areas of your business that are less sexy is important (especially if you don't have the funds to pay someone else to do it *yet*).

Let's begin to put this chapter into action! First, brainstorm a list of decisions or tasks you perform for your side hustle. Next, identify the current decision-making approach you use. Now consider which of the approaches listed below may be more optimal. For example, we were considering starting a podcast but didn't have the time to manage all the back-end work, so we hired a firm to handle this for us (**outsource**). Or, we often like to work late at night but found that editing a book needed our best hours of the day (**peak performance**).

DECISIONS/TASKS:	CURRENT APPROACH:	*OPTIMAL APPOACH:*
1.		
2.		
3.		
4.		
5.		
6.		
7.		
8.		
9.		
10.		

DECISION-MAKING APPROACHES:

- **Peak Performance:** Important and requires your best working hours.
- **Non-Peak Performance**: Necessary and can be done any time, or is a low priority.
- **Consult Expert**: Important and too complex to make on your own.
- **Develop Skill/Expertise**: Important area to grow your knowledge.
- **Intuition**: Your experience allows for quick execution even with high stakes.
- **Execute Quickly**: Outcome is low stakes.
- **Delegate**: Can be done by someone else within your team or business.
- **Outsource**: Can be sent to a virtual assistant, contractor or vendor.
- **Automate**: Determine how to streamline.
- **Unnecessary**: Doesn't need to be executed at all.

— — —

By remembering to consider all the various options and approaches available for any particular task or challenge, you will develop more awareness around your decision making and you can continue to strike a balance between being indecisive or too hasty. When you can switch gears and effectively apply analytics as well as be decisive in your action, you will have the foundational skills necessary for more competent decision making. Over time this balance and experience will lend way to developing strong instincts.

So a hearty cheers to making strong, confident, balanced decisions! And speaking of commitment, let's dial forward to some of the most important decisions you face as a business owner—building your inner circle, your team, the WHO within your business, those responsible for helping you create the side hustle success we know is so valuable.

CHAPTER 9

Selecting Your Inner Circle

Diving Deeper into the WHO

*We can see that all the desirable
experiences that we cherish or aspire to
attain are dependent upon cooperation and
interaction with other sentient beings.*
—Dalai Lama

In Chapter 3, "The WHO," we discussed the necessity of selecting the right people to associate with, people who support your lifestyle and ambitions and can help pull you forward. By now, hopefully you are beyond the planning stage, which means selecting or hiring an inner circle who will help you grow and operate the different functions of your business. *WHO* you choose to go into business with, take council from, and hire can make or break you. And side hustlers often make some common mistakes in this area that we would like to help you avoid.

First, when starting a side hustle, it's important to take inventory of your own skills, strengths, weaknesses, likes, and dislikes, so you can properly offset them with other business partners, employees, professionals, or vendors. Everyone has blind spots, and surrounding ourselves with top-level experts or those highly skilled where a person may easily fumble can make a business excel that would otherwise flounder.

Second, aspiring business owners often make the mistake of basing these crucial decisions exclusively on who they already know or like without evaluating essential characteristics that their current sphere of influence may or may not have. This chapter teaches you how and why to expand your scope of selection along with how to better evaluate your potential inner circle.

The Function of Your Inner Circle

While it goes beyond the scope of this book to help you identify all your advantages and limitations, we have listed some critical components of a side hustle that we have found are necessary for success. In the event you have some glaring shortcomings, consider some of the following relationships to offset your weaknesses, preferably proactively! Michael Gerber, author of *The E-Myth Revisited: Why Most Small Business Don't Work and What to Do About It*, shares that every successful business has three key personnel: the entrepreneur, the technician, and the manager. Most people are strong in one department, mediocre in another, and weak in the third.

Common side hustle duties include sales, marketing, advertising, accounting, operations, product development and distribution, inventory management, customer relations, social media, PR, public speaking, networking, website management, and others. So begin by asking yourself which items on this list energize you, what can you live with doing, what do you loathe, and what, if any, are you flat-out incompetent or unwilling to do? Depending on your answers and their corresponding severity, there are different inner-circle relationships you should forge to balance these weaknesses.

Partnerships

When you find a solid business partner you diversify everything: ownership, investment, risk, skills, perspective, and of course, *profit*. You can create an immense amount of leverage by having other people with strong expertise and skills who also have skin in the game. Partners are particularly useful when you have major ongoing constraints such as capital, time, or a key technical expertise. Also note, business partnership arrangements can be of varying splits. Everything we own together is 50/50. We recently bought a lake house, which we occasionally use as a short-term rental, and went in 50/50 with some other business partners, but ownership doesn't *have* to be equally divided. We have seen successful partnerships with 25/75 or even 1/99 splits! *Just make sure each person has a clearly defined role and corresponding responsibilities to avoid confusion.*

Contractors

These are typically individuals you bring in for a set amount of work to handle a specific project: web developers, virtual assistants, design consultants, and so on. Many people can build their own website (if they are willing to invest the time) or design their own logo, but oftentimes hiring an expert can be both more efficient and effective than fumbling around with a graphic design software you don't understand as you attempt to create a polished end product. If necessary, circle back to our last chapter on decision making for additional support.

Professional Advisors

When you just need a specific type of advice on occasion, or a few times a year, this is a great type of relationship to have. We discuss how to identify these advisors—CPAs, attorneys, wealth advisors, insurance specialists—later in this chapter.

Employees

We placed employees last because most side hustlers are not as interested in fronting the necessary capital it requires to finance someone else's job if they haven't generated enough cash to replace their own. There are exceptions, of course. However, the great advantages of having (well-chosen) employees are:

- ▶ They can often perform a wide range of tasks and can provide air coverage for areas of your business that you don't have the time or energy to manage.
- ▶ They can completely take things off your plate and buy back time into your life or business to focus on the things that matter more or only you can do.

▶ They can be fluid in their role. Once you train an employee, you can create a large return on having someone equipped and anchored internally.

▶ They bring new, fresh perspectives and expertise with the interest of the company in mind. An employee likely won't be as invested as the owner or a partner; however, if carefully selected and compensated, they can add additional horsepower to the growth of the firm.

Curating Your Inner Circle: Deciding Who Makes the Cut

Your capacity to interview and evaluate character, motivation, resourcefulness, competency, and personality can flip the scale on creating a successful relationship versus a painful misfire. As you strengthen your ability to assess the core qualities that are required of successful business relationships, you will experience greater continuity and health in your growth.

There are many things at stake when you pull people around a business plan with the intention of creating growth—your time, money, livelihood, and reputation. When deciding who makes the cut, we advise considering many factors beyond just skill or likeability.

Character

This is by far the most important factor to consider when selecting a potential business partner or employee. Great skill, likability, and work ethic are valuable, but they are multiplied by *zero* if someone's character or integrity are weak. A few ways to confirm good character: What does their work history look like? Have they shown consistency, or has there consistently been issues? Does drama follow them like a Wisconsin midsummer mosquito? Have they received increased responsibility in their work history?

Craig here. A couple years ago, I invested in a firm that was already doing over $1 million in revenue with good net profit. I knew two of the three partners. I took a minority percentage for a modest but not insignificant investment and planned to be a passive investor and advisor. I would support them when I could with referrals, banking, budgeting, and financial advice. One of the partners had a traditional business that was small but performing well. He was good friends and long-term business partners with another gentleman who had a strong IT background and a large family business he helped support. There was a third partner, the founder of the business, whom I did not know, but for whom both the people I knew vouched for.

Prior to investing I called four people for advice, and here is what they shared. I am paraphrasing their responses:

"I never get into any business unless I have majority of the control. Otherwise, somebody else will mess it up and I always trust myself more than others." (owner of a dozen companies and a multi-decamillionaire by 38)

"Sure, if you *want*. Just don't *lose* or commit any *time*. I know one of those guys. I'm sure they are good people." (multimillionaire mentor of ours for 15 years and world-class public speaker)

"If you think the business and investment is a good idea. It's your money you have saved from your days as a GE employee. How much will you go in for?" (Carrie)

"Huh. Sounds interesting. So you know two of the three guys? Just make sure you feel comfortable with the third partner, especially if he is the technician, founder, and primary operator." (owner and operator of a sizable real estate agency and nonprofit).

I decided to invest the money. Against some of the advice I received, I did *not* gain majority control and invested double my initial threshold of comfort. I did *not* properly vet the third partner (this was my biggest mistake). I also invested some time, but it was limited (thank goodness for my mentor's suggestion as I set pretty strong boundaries around this).

Within six months the company was no longer *operational*, let alone profitable. After 12 months none of the other three partners would have conversations with each other. Now several years later, the firm still hasn't yet filed for bankruptcy, let alone paid out any distributions. I lost everything (well, except a capital loss deduction on our taxes).

As painful and expensive as a lesson like that can be, I *learned a ton* (remember our antifragile self-image from Chapter 6) about myself, about investing, and about people. Just because I was a banker, knew how to shred a financial statement, made other smart investments, and had other businesses did *not guarantee success in a new environment*. Interestingly, in my emotionally charged haste I had broken several of my own investing rules.

Had I looked deeper into the relationships of the primary owner, I would have discovered a lack of continuity, several prior busted business partnerships, broken personal relationships, and a shortfall of objective references. How someone has conducted themselves with other people matters. If you can't confirm solid references, consider partnering with someone else, or limit the scope or responsibilities of the individual in question.

In addition, what good was all that great mentorship and advice I received if I wasn't willing to apply it? There is nothing more frustrating for a mentor than to provide council to someone in good faith, knowing it will be extremely valuable, only to have the mentee not apply the advice and fail in the process.

Financial Resources

A potential business partner's financial strength is not the only factor to consider, but it is relevant. We are not going to imply someone must have strong financial resources to start a business or be a good partner—many entrepreneurs do not! But if someone is financially destitute, it doesn't give them or *you* a lot of cushion if things do get tough financially (and they invariably will). The financial responsibility will fall squarely on your shoulders. If they are not young, a deeper concern would be *why* are they still financially struggling? What is the quality of their thinking related to money management? *If* they do have resources, what is their motivation for going into business?

Motivation

Why someone may be getting into business with you is an important factor to understand. Here are a few questions you can ask yourself (or them, when reasonable). Many of these items can be stress tested by simply seeing the potential partner's past behavior, asking these questions, or getting to know them or former associates over time.

▶ Why are they getting into business with you? Are they someday planning to take over their parents' multimillion-dollar business, and this will be a fun little temporary project for them? Or are they financially desperate and need to make some cash ASAP?

▶ Does their Lifeset look good, meaning does it appear they have healthy long-term professional and personal relationships in their life?

▶ Do they have a history of being an "idea" person and hop from project to project? Many pseudo-entrepreneurs have brilliant ideas but couldn't put a balance sheet together, let alone a functioning business, if their life was at stake.

▶ Are they addicted to the rush of doing something *new* and to the *notion* of entrepreneurship, not entrepreneurship itself?

▶ Are they motivated because they sense you are already on the way up and can take them to the promised land? This is not necessarily a negative motivation; just make sure they are also willing to do the work to help you get there.

You can go into business with someone even if they are not a model citizen. They don't need to take a lie detector test to confirm their motivation. But again, past behavioral patterns leave clues.

A successful entrepreneur we know was asked to participate in a very large real estate deal with some big-time players. He ended up backing out of the deal—not because he didn't think it was good, but because all the other players involved were significantly further along financially. He wondered, why did they need his few hundred thousand when they were investing tens of millions? Something about people worth hundreds of millions asking him to get in just didn't feel quite right. Because this entrepreneur, who already had numerous successful business partnerships, couldn't understand the motivation behind their behavior, he decided to pass on the deal. He was thankful, as several years later two of the partners filed for bankruptcy. He never found out what the real issue was, but the entrepreneur we know was glad he took a pass.

Creating Balance and Offsetting Your Weaknesses

So many reasons to develop business partnerships are because someone can bring a strength to a company or team that you may not have. It could be financial, technical, or industry connections, etc. Introspection and understanding your own deficiencies are critical because they help you identify what talents you need on board and solicit them. A few questions you should ask yourself and them: What is the actual value they bring to the table? Is the value worth the ownership percentage or compensation they will acquire? What tangible resources or skills have they already demonstrated in their work history?

What do *you* bring to the table? Is it proportional to your contribution and does it line up with your ownership equitably? *If not, it is likely just a matter of time before either one of you feel underpaid—or the other partners do.*

Creating partnerships that complement each other is smart business strategy. If your potential partner or employee's primary strength is creativity, but they are weak in processes or management, are you capable of bridging that gap or are you also totally incompetent in those areas? If you are strong at initiating or starting connections, is your potential partner a strong closer?

For instance, Craig here. Carrie knows if I'm on a call and there are certain things I say I will execute on a follow-up task when the call ends, there is a good chance I will *not follow through* in a reasonable time frame. It's not that I'm lazy; trust me, I am nothing of the sort! My ADHD brain just naturally flows to the next shiny object at hand, and the simplest of items are temporarily (or sometime permanently) forgotten. She has learned not to count on me for that type of immediate follow-through and has luckily stepped up and overcompensated for my incompetence in this regard (and many others).

As another example, we know someone who runs a small retail business. One partner is an excellent salesman, and the other is brilliant with management and accounting. It's the classic business partnership really. It works well for them and they don't seem to judge one another for the strengths or weaknesses they have. It's a great example of an effective *inter-dependent relationship*.

Personality

Unfortunately, most newly minted business owners make the mistake of leading with this when it comes to choosing who they go into business with. **Enjoying someone's company is a radically different experience than building a company;** they are two totally different buckets. Just ask *any* married couple in business together.

We often jest about our differences in how we choose our healthcare providers. Carrie places a strong emphasis on how much she *likes* the medical professionals who have helped her on her health journey. She falls hard and fast for those who express great empathy, are kind, and build rapport. Craig is all for doctors and nurses having a wonderful bedside manner—but if it comes down to kindness *or* competence, Craig would choose competence *every single time*. The preference is to find both, of course!

But how nice someone is, is not always a good determinant of their technical competence or character. So many times, we have heard the statement, "Oh my financial planner, they are a great friend!" That's fine. But if they are charging you excessive fees for your $250,000 in assets under management, putting your investments in heavily loaded and underperforming mutual funds (because there is extra commission), and overselling you whole or permanent life insurance, I'd say fire them and find someone competent. Or at least find someone with good pricing. Unless, of course, them being a "great friend" is worth thousands of dollars per year to you.

Learn to Draft Your Team Instead of Recruit

Explore. Check your options. This can help give you a much stronger perspective on moving forward by validating you got the best deal in town (or on Zoom). Having options can also give you better negotiating power.

One of the best areas we "invested" in a couple years ago was getting an au pair (aka a live-in nanny) from Colombia. Some people close to us were initially confused by this. We had someone ask us, "So she is going to like . . . *live* in your house?" None of our peers had used an au pair before, but we wanted to give it a go for a few reasons: we were paying about the same amount of money for a lot *less* childcare, we wanted our children to learn some Spanish and gain exposure to another language and culture firsthand, and we wanted to provide a great experience for someone who loved children and desired an opportunity to come to the States.

> **It's important to interview more than one candidate before you settle on a random business partner, vendor, mentor, or spouse. *Remember, Think NBA drafting, not collegiate recruiting.***

When we started the interviewing process, we conducted over a dozen interviews. We went back and forth between our top couple selections and eventually extended an offer to Isa. She accepted, and it has worked out wonderfully—she is now completing her *second* year in our home. We are in the process of helping her apply for a master's program to extend her time in the United States. She has become our fifth family member. Now, honestly, there is some luck involved in finding a great match, but we were surprised to hear how many of these pairings don't go well. We asked several people how many nannies they interviewed, and someone responded, "You mean, you interviewed more than one?" Choosing an individual to live with our family was an extensive vetting process. Why would you let someone become a business partner in a major area of your life without a strong selection process?

So you mean to say you are going to start your first business; invest hours of time, sweat, blood, and your hard-earned capital; and not going to consider interviewing any other options for your possible business partner?

It's important to note that the preceding recommendations are not hard lined. We *all* bring weaknesses and past mistakes to any venture. These are simply important things to consider prior to starting a business or bringing on a new supplier or relationship.

We have witnessed a large number of entrepreneurs who would have been considerably better off, and happier human beings, had they asked these questions.

Choosing Your Professional Advisors

Although much of the preceding information already applies when choosing which professionals to work with, here are a few additional thoughts to consider when hiring the following:

Bank, banker

Attorney

Accountant

Marketing, advertising company

Financial advisor

Contractor, realtor

Consulting for social media, advertising, IT, etc.

When choosing these professionals, consider whether they are generalists or if they specialize in your industry. Is it important to you to have a specialist? What phase of their career are they in? For example, you can find an accountant right out of college who may be economical, but if they haven't handled more sophisticated taxes for businesses, they might not be your best option. You can also find an attorney or an accountant who is extremely sophisticated but at a premium price that may be unnecessary for some basic contract or legal work. Just because you know a bankruptcy attorney who works in contract law, doesn't mean you want to hire them to advise you on a complicated intellectual property issue. With attorneys this is fairly obvious, but with many other professionals they might not always volunteer their experience or credibility unless you ask. Not all CPAs, financial advisors, and attorneys are created equal, so when possible get referrals from other business owners or contacts you know and trust.

Selecting Vendors, Suppliers, and Other B2B Relationships

A few additional things to consider when deciding between vendors, suppliers, and other business-to-business relationships.

What is the firm's reputation in the industry? Have you even cross-referenced or checked? Ask their other customers what the firm is like to work with!

What are the vendor's typical terms of paying their customers or suppliers? Depending on the amount of the contract involved you can run a

Dun & Bradstreet Report, which provides some of this type of information. Consider running a *pilot* order through a vendor. This allows a test run and lets the vendor know you are serious about receiving a quality service or product before you go all in with them.

Set expectations *clearly and establish a legal contract as necessary,* so as to avoid any confusion later. If needed, have a trusted attorney create or review large contracts. *Never* be afraid to shop for a better deal—even just to keep your current supplier *honest.* Taking 20 minutes and making a couple quick phone calls (or having an employee do so) to cross-reference your pricing can oftentimes provide a lot of leverage.

Recently we had to hire an attorney to review some contracts. The attorney we worked with a few years ago was solid and came highly recommended, but was extremely hard to get a hold of and in process of phasing out of his career. We got a referral from a trusted business partner for an alternate option. The potential attorney's pricing was good, but we were not comfortable with their communication style or background. So we ended up with an attorney who has done more sophisticated work in the areas we needed support in. At $500 an hour, it cost us $1,000 to have them review two contracts, but in the end we felt comfortable with the quality of the work.

As a business owner, you can shop almost all services and negotiate many of them. **Negotiating pricing is more common as a business owner, as the transactions are larger and vendors generally have fewer clients, giving you more leverage.** *Don't be afraid to challenge for the best pricing*—especially if your business is on a tight budget. Of course, don't be a jerk or challenge their pricing in *every* conversation, but smart business owners are skilled at receiving the value they are paying for.

— — —

People often ask us (generally individually) how we like running a business with our spouse. Sometimes they scoff and say, "Well, I could never run a business with my husband." We have been fortunate in our partnership as we both took careful inventory early on to make sure we had a strong enough alignment in the areas covered in this chapter to actually be successful together. Whichever side hustle you choose and whoever you choose to accompany you, take your time—choose wisely. Making smart selections in this department can propel your side hustle forward in big ways, and good choices also make the adventure much more enjoyable!

CHAPTER 10

Funding Your Venture

If you are smart, you are going to make
a lot of money without borrowing. I've
never borrowed a significant amount of
money in my life. Never. Never will.
—Warren Buffett

Funding your side hustle is a necessity. Sure, everyone's read the romantic stories about the millionaire who began a company with five dollars to their name; however, relying on stories about such outliers is not realistic or helpful. Whether you are thinking about putting your savings in, borrowing from a relative at a low interest rate, or going to a local credit union or large bank, this chapter helps you make critical decisions about funding your venture. The stronger your resources at the start and the better plan you put in place, the more likely you are to weather the challenging times and pull through victorious.

The best high-level advice we can provide when it comes to funding your venture is to make sure you consider *multiple options*, especially prior to borrowing money. We have seen many business owners acquire credit by advancing on their credit cards or using high-interest lenders when there was a more cost-effective loan available to them at their local bank. There are different sources of funding, and we help you compare and contrast those differences, so you can make smart decisions. If you read the last chapter, you probably have access to an accountant and/or financial professional you trust, so it's a good idea to consult them when making your funding decisions, especially if you are looking to inject or borrow large amounts of money.

Typically, there are four ways to raise capital for your business: injecting personal cash, borrowing or debt, selling equity or ownership, and creating additional sources of revenue.

Note: This chapter is designed to provide a *practical overview*, sufficient for most side hustlers. But if you are looking to inject or borrow large amounts of money, we recommend getting a second opinion from a trusted source such as a credible mentor, banker, financier, consultant, CPA, or successful business owner. As business owners, people are often so emotionally wrapped up in their own companies that they fail to clearly see major blind spots easily seen or spotted by others, especially when it comes to money.

Option 1: Personal Cash Injections

Many people start small businesses (especially side hustlers) by injecting money from their own pocketbook. This money could be used for anything from buying a new laptop, licensing, office space, building a website, or Facebook advertising. When it comes to investing your own money in a side hustle, consider the following:

▸ **Track the dollars invested.** This is important for accounting purposes and making sure you have a clear understanding of how your business is actually performing. It is also helpful as you complete your taxes every year so you can maximize your deductions and provide accurate data. We have always worked to provide accurate and honest information when filing our taxes. Sleeping well at night is a part of our Life Vision. Cutting corners to save a few dollars on your tax return is not worth the paranoia that the IRS will call you out someday or the breach of your own personal integrity.

▸ **Create a budget and projections—and manage to them.** Using the personal budget we discussed in Chapter 4, "Lifeset," develop a general budget or dollar amount that you feel comfortable with investing into your side hustle at the outset of your business plan.

In addition to basic budgeting, we recommend creating projections for your business. This challenges you to forecast both your sales revenue *and* your anticipated expenses. Make sure to also have a contingency plan in place in the event more capital is needed because revenue or expenses do not line up perfectly with your projections (they rarely do). It is nearly impossible for entrepreneurs to forecast all the possible monetary variables that can arise as additional services, equipment, and tools are needed. Last, update your budget and projections monthly or quarterly. Many never put solid projections together, but for those who do, even fewer use them as a real tool to manage their business. Don't be one of them!

▶ **Establish a stable financial situation.** Remember why we invested so much time into your finances and career in the chapter on Lifeset? Whether it's your day job, another business, or savings, make sure you have consistent money to draw from to both live your life and properly manage your business in a *sustainable way*. Many great businesses have died on the runway because they could afford to buy the jet but then simply did not have enough money to get that jet in the air—or keep it in the air!

▶ **Understand your risk tolerance and be mindful of the "law of sunken costs."** How much money are you willing to invest or can you afford to lose? How much can you invest and *for how long*? The law of sunk costs refers to continuing to invest into an endeavor (even if it is going to fail) just because you have already invested money or resources. Again, when you have breathed life into your business and invested sweat, tears, and blood, you might be too involved and it can be helpful to step back and get the perspective of a consultant or other qualified individual.

Option 2: Borrowing 102

As a side hustler there is a good chance you may not have to play the borrowing game at all, at least initially. However, as your side hustle grows, borrowing money may either became a necessity or present a massive opportunity to go to the next level and/or convert to a front hustle.

Being a former banker (essentially a professional money lender), Craig has seen many people use borrowing as a tool to enhance their leverage and wealth. We have also seen many entrepreneurs borrow money with the right intentions but end up getting themselves into a *world of hurt*. Before you ever borrow from family, friends, banks, or other financial institutions, it is important to understand *why* your company needs to borrow money so you can properly match the right kind of loans to it. Meaning, do you need to borrow funds for purchasing new equipment, a marketing campaign, product development, hiring an employee, office space, or purchasing a building? Clearly understanding *why* you want the money is important to identify so you can also confirm *if* you need it or if you can get by without it.

In general, we recommend borrowing only as needed because borrowing money means you are taking on some form of debt or a loan and any interest you pay is an expense that ultimately comes off your revenue and reduces your profit. Many businesses (just like individuals) have to spend much of their hard-earned revenue to pay for interest. We personally would rather keep our profit, and we prefer you do also. For instance, we have seen many people rack up consumer credit card debt to fund excess inventory purchasing or marketing services when they didn't have enough infrastructure like a strong website or sales pipeline to justify the purchase. Six months later their naive thinking and weak planning has them $40,000 in credit card debt and no clear plan to move the inventory.

However, there is no doubt that borrowing can create a positive form of leverage, because doing so lets you expand, buy new equipment, or add a location that can eventually generate far more profit than the interest the loan may cost.

There are many different ways to borrow money along with many different reasons, both positive and negative. If you don't have a background in finance, we want to help you navigate this terrain effectively. Let's begin by taking a look at two very simple ways to categorize most loans and the most common types of lenders.

1. **Term loan.** This type of loan is much like a mortgage on a home. It has a set principal amount up front and generally a set monthly payment and fixed interest rate. These loans usually amortize (reduce the amount you owe by paying on a schedule) the initial borrowing amount down to zero over a 5-, 10-, 20-, or 30-year

period. However, some notes have balloon payments, meaning you might make payments for five years and still have a large amount of principal owed at the end. Term loans are generally used to finance such items such as real estate or equipment.

2. **Line of credit.** This type of loan works more like a credit card with a credit limit. If you have a $20,000 line of credit with the bank, you can borrow against it whenever you wish and pay it off whenever you choose. It is more customizable, as you may borrow from the line of credit for a large inventory purchase, but then pay off the balance as soon as you have sold the inventory. You are charged interest, but only for the amount of principal and how long you borrowed it for. This type of loan is generally used to finance inventory or accounts receivables.

Different Types of Lenders

1. Family and Friends

Many great businesses have been started by a handshake and a small loan from a loved one. If the interest rate and terms are reasonable, this is a perfectly viable route. We do recommend establishing clear terms and documenting the loan for all parties involved. Make sure both parties have a good understanding of a realistic payment schedule. Also, it is wise to understand the lender's (your friend's) financial situation. Does this money *need* to be paid back in 12 months, or is the timeline more flexible as they have millions in savings and lending you $10,000 doesn't really impact them?

In the event your business is in a jam or needs capital, sucking up your ego and calling a good friend or loved one is oftentimes a better play than borrowing money at extremely high interest rates or terms from some of the following lenders, especially the nontraditional ones.

2. Banks and Credit Unions

Unless you're getting favorable terms from a friend or your network, banks and credit unions are generally the best place to start when seeking out a business loan. They usually provide the best interest rates and lowest fee structures. However, they tend to be the most conservative (least likely to lend) and require you to prove your business's profitability and capacity to pay back the loan.

Most banks are relatively good at determining why you need a loan, and they will likely collateralize it with particular assets such as real estate, inventory, accounts receivable, and so on. However, many people borrow or raise money for the right reason—but then use the funds incorrectly.

Craig once created a $100,000 line of credit for a profitable flooring business run by a husband-and-wife team. The loan was essentially for financing inventory. However, right after the loan was approved, the company added a couple employees. Then simultaneously and unexpectedly their revenue dropped. They started borrowing money from their line of credit and eventually maxed it out, asking the bank for a credit line increase. When we asked them to show their inventory levels, they had only $20,000, not the $100,000 borrowed! They had been paying the new employees' salaries with the line of credit, instead of using it to cover inventory. They had no way to pay down the loan and had to sell off one of their locations and some real estate just to stay afloat and pay back the bank. This also wreaked havoc on the two owners' personal lives; they were married when they got the loan but divorced by the time the loan was paid back.

You *do not* want to borrow money to fund operating losses when the money has been borrowed for other purposes such as inventory, new equipment, accounts receivable, and so on. Many small business owners innocently take out a small line of capital or borrow money on a credit card to cover extraordinary expenses and end up covering bad losses without realizing it. This can be hard to recover from and difficult to detect if you are not watching cash flow closely. If you do not have a background in accounting or finance or do not have a particular aptitude for tracking cash flow, hire someone periodically to do so.

3. The Government

Several government programs are available and sometimes local or regional programs are as well. In the event these loans provide truly favorable terms, such as grants or subsidized interest rates, they can be a good option. However, oftentimes these loans can be stacked with fees or other stipulations that might offset any type of initial attractive interest rates. Small Business Administration (SBA) loans that have fees, while providing low interest rates, are often not as favorable as acquiring a straight bank loan.

4. Alternative Borrowing Options

People also borrow from alternative sources such as PayPal, Payday Loans, cash advances on credit cards, factoring (accounts receivable financing), or even loan sharks (aka Shylocks if you keep up on your Shakespeare) when a bank loan is not viable. This generally occurs because the business owner doesn't have strong enough finances or credit rating to acquire a bank loan. As a result, these alternative institutions or individuals do not typically offer as favorable of terms as a friend, bank, or credit union. Rates, fees, or both are typically higher since people defer to these organizations oftentimes out of desperation. However, these organizations do vary from reasonable and helpful to downright ridiculous.

An example is factoring, which is borrowing money against future customer orders for which you have not been paid. Factoring companies lend you money based on your accounts receivable (A/R). The loans often charge interest between 10 and 30 percent for financing, and we would only recommend using these rates in the most desperate of times.

Rather than considering these options, you are oftentimes better off getting more creative by taking out a personal home equity line of credit (HELOC), an advance on a low-interest credit card, that friendly loan from Grandpa, or other options that cost significantly less in the end.

If you are the *only* person with access to capital or credit, the pressure to produce the funds rests squarely on your shoulders in times of difficulty or expansion. All the more reason to choose your business partners wisely, as discussed in Chapter 9, "Selecting Your Inner Circle."

Option 3: Selling Equity or Ownership

Selling shares or ownership of your company is another viable way of raising capital. Although we have invested in several companies as minority owners and supported other businesses in selling equity, we have not personally sold equity to fund our businesses. However, relying on Craig's former banking experience and our combined investor background, here are a few tips we can offer:

- ▸ **Raise enough funds on the first round to provide a strong cushion.** This can help you avoid having to sell another round of shares and minimize any midterm cash crunches.
- ▸ **Find investors who can also be an asset to your business by becoming an advisor or providing other relevant technical expertise.** These "advisors" are also *vested* in your success and should provide sound or quality advice, resources, or relationships as needed.
- ▸ **Make sure you have an experienced attorney and CPA assisting you with selling equity in your firm.** It is not advisable to go raise capital by selling your equity without professional guidance.
- ▸ **Consider other forms of raising capital first!** Rather than selling ownership in your business, does it make more sense to sell that RV, land, or cabin you rarely use? Or does it make sense to borrow from a bank or other source?

Option 4: Creating New Revenue Sources

Raising funds by increasing revenue is another option many small business owners overlook! In his career, there were *several times* Craig had to decline loans to business owners and it often forced the business owners to step up their games. Those were never fun conversations to have and often difficult messages to deliver. However, here are some of the things we have witnessed business owners do when they had maxed out their borrowing capacity and were *forced* to innovate:

- ▸ **Raise pricing on a product or services.** Customers may not always like it, but they often understand that slow levels of increased pricing is normal and can be driven by general inflation or other operating cost increases. Small and incremental price increases are less jarring to your customer base and more readily accepted than waiting five years, hitting the panic button, and shocking your customers with a 50 percent price increase so you can stay afloat. Plan ahead, look at your projections, and watch the costs of your vendors and suppliers. As they adjust, consider adjusting accordingly. *Have the confidence that your services are worth paying for.*

▶ **Add *new* fees for current services or products you already provide.** For example, if you run a coaching business and often evaluate business plans for free, why not create this option as its own add-on service fee? You know it adds a *ton* of value for your client, and you can now get compensated for the value you are delivering. Or what if you are a social media consultant and provide consulting across all major platforms? Perhaps you can provide standard pricing for three or four platforms and charge an additional fee to add Pinterest or TikTok.

▶ **Add *new* products or services.** Innovate! Is there something you could easily add to your suite of services and attach a cost? If so, make it happen! For example, if you're an automotive station and you already vacuum cars before giving them back to the clients, can you take it up a couple of notches and provide detailed cleaning? You may already have the employees in place with some idle downtime and likely most of the equipment you need. This could be a way to add real margin to your bottom line. There are usually countless opportunities to add new services. A great way to identify these is ask or study other businesses in your industry. Are they charging for a service you could easily add?

▶ **Sell out any old inventory or current inventory at a discount.** As mentioned earlier, blowing out old inventory is a beautiful way to raise some cash and save on space. Carrie here. I have been on one of my Marie Kondo benders lately and as a result, I've sold the most random things in our house and raised a couple thousand in cash. Keep in mind, most things that work for your business can also work for your personal economy—and vice versa!

▶ **Look for other places to cut costs and increase efficiencies** such as a reduction of store hours, sectioning off a portion of your facility for someone else to rent, or eliminating other service memberships or fees your business is paying for but isn't really using. One thing COVID-19 times taught us is to innovate, and many costs such as office space may not be as necessary as we all thought.

During Craig's last year working in banking he had to deliver a very difficult message to one of his good customers, who was also a friend. The business owner had requested a $500,000 loan but the bank declined it.

The business had already borrowed too much money and was overleveraged. The owner took it personally and was visibly upset with Craig and the bank. However, the owner rose to the occasion, cut back on store hours, blew out some old inventory, and let go of some staff members (staff he should have cut back on years ago). The business got lean and back to a place of profitability. Interestingly, the lack of additional capital put the right pressure on him to go perform and ultimately run a more healthy and profitable business. As much as he was frustrated with the bank for declining the loan, it was the right decision and on some level the owner was appreciative. Just borrowing more money would have supported the weak, unprofitable business practices and not have forced change and innovation.

You may not need to borrow that much money or inject that much cash to grow your side hustle. But as you do grow, be mindful of what different costs, products, or pricing you can adjust, rather than simply injecting more time or money without evaluating why.

– – –

Being a good entrepreneur often requires being entrepreneurial about how to acquire new money or how to better manage the funds you have.

Interestingly, we see many small business owners who are willing to be innovative about their specific product or service, but then not about how they manage or finance their business. You can have the greatest product in the world, but if you run out of the money to provide it, you won't be in business for long.

CHAPTER 11

Marketing and Branding Your Side Hustle

Your brand is a gateway to your true work.
—Dave Buck

As a side hustler, learning how to effectively market your business is crucial, as you don't exist without sales and revenue. Your business name, logo, packaging, slogan or tagline, hashtag on social media, and mission statement on your website are tools. Keep in mind, for most side hustlers the primary purpose of these marketing tools is to create revenue. In today's times you also have access to additional marketing strategies such as paid advertisements, sales funnels, pay per click, podcasting, SEO (search engine optimization), content marketing, and campaigns. These tools and strategies are *amplified* by your brand. Your business brand is at the heart of your marketing, and as a solopreneur, you also have a personal brand, which is comprised of, well, you. As an individual who is also a business owner there is a *strong* intersection of your personal brand and your business brand. We explore this relationship and help you strategize how to grow as you market both yourself and your business.

As a side hustler, you are the face of your business and brand; you are the ambassador. What you personally value gets translated into your business, and vice versa. The personal and business brands for some of the most effective business owners are interchangeable and almost indistinguishable from one another. They are one.

When we examine the large-scale enterprises of Ray Dalio, Beyonce, and Seth Godin, it is clear their businesses are anchored in the personal brand of each individual. When you think of their companies, you see their face and you remember their story. They have mastered the art of weaving themselves throughout their business brand—and it is immensely powerful.

On the flip side, if there is incongruence between someone's personal brand and their company's brand, you are likely not drawn to that business or compelled to support it. Again, since the personal brand can amplify your business brand, it can also damage it.

This demonstrates the importance of brand consistency. Consistency in a world of disruption is difficult but ever-more important. A solid brand takes on an identity of its own and makes a product or service identifiable and distinguishable. And when you are consistent, people tend to trust and rely on you more.

But I'm not Gary V. or Oprah, do I really need to brand myself to have a successful side hustle? Heck yes! Here is why—people's purchase decisions are made as much based on branding as they are on the product and service itself.

When you see a modern apple silhouette, we globally think of one of the world's most valuable brands, Apple Inc. It could be a sticker on a dumpster, but you still associate the symbol with the tech empire. For many though, the Apple brand represents more than just a technology device; it stands for cutting edge, creative, and forward thinking. And by buying an Apple product you are saying to the world, I am these things! People often don't want to admit it, but they spend money and buy things that are consistent with how they want to be perceived by the world around them. Apple spends millions of dollars on marketing to make you feel a certain way when you see and use their products. This is the essence of branding and Apple has mastered it.

Now as a side hustler, you don't have to spend millions on commercial spots, but you can take a cue from what major companies do and make it a priority that your branding have a similar effect. Ultimately, this branding example embodies the art of differentiation, as branding guru David Brier describes in his book *Brand Intervention*, which should be the goal of any company large or small. If people know who you are and how you make them feel, you can differentiate yourself and your business.

The reality is if you exist in the twenty-first century as an individual or a business, you have a brand, it just might not be intentional—yet. As discussed in Chapter 6, we all have a brand. Even your mom has a brand. How she dresses, communicates, what she stands for, where she invests her time, and so on. This brand impacts how you and others respond to her. As Jeff Bezos famously said, "Your brand is what people say about you when you're not in the room," and an effective brand can be described with just a few primary adjectives. Identifying what those qualities, strengths, and characteristics are for your brand helps you define distinctly how you want to resonate with others and how they think of you.

When we think about the small business owners and side hustlers whom we love doing business with and refer others to, there are common reasons. These owners are often known for being honest, genuine, humble; they overdeliver and are focused on the long game and do the right thing long-term for their clients. They are effective at sales, without being salesy. Branding is about creating a reputation that precedes you and communicating it so clearly it sticks.

If your audience doesn't *trust* you, and your strategies are ineffective, then it will be very difficult for your business to take flight. Many people ask, "If a brand is so important, where do I start?" This chapter provides you with a high-level crash course to instill helpful thought processes when it comes to building your brand. We discuss a number of different avenues for effective business and personal branding as you scale your side business, but the major takeaways are understanding your audience, building your story, creating content, and developing a plan to have that content reach your target audience. Further, we discuss the fundamentals of building a following on social media, effective networking, and creating revenue through marketing strategies. Some of these steps may feel beyond where you are currently, but they are all good to keep top of mind for your future success.

Understand Your Audience

There is a saying in marketing, "If you try to talk to everyone, you wind up reaching no one." Knowing your target audience is critical to your success. If you don't identify who you are trying to reach, it's going to be hard to, well, reach them. *Everyone is not your audience.* In fact, when you are vague on who your audience is, there is a lot of lost opportunity as you won't be able to effectively zoom in and connect with the individuals or groups that actually are. By getting specific you can invest the majority of your resources and efforts into resonating with the right people.

Questions to Ask to Target Your Market

▶ What are their needs and pain points?
▶ What problems are you able to help them solve?
▶ What demographic are they a part of?
▶ What types of aesthetics are they drawn to? For example, style, colors, imagery, etc.
▶ What are their habits?
▶ How do they spend their time? What does a day in the life look like?
▶ What are their psychographics, meaning what are their motivations, behaviors, and attitudes? What are their rational and irrational motivations, behaviors, and attitudes? For example, do they want a powerful car, or do they want to appear powerful to their friends?
▶ What inspires them?
▶ What type of content do they consume?
▶ What genre of podcasts do they listen to?
▶ Where do they show up? Are they on social media? If so, TikTok or Instagram? LinkedIn or Facebook? All of the above?

Your answers to these questions inform the kind of content you generate along with a solid basis for reverse engineering a plan for effective branding. If you already have revenue flowing, take a look at your current clients; they can give you very helpful insight into the previous questions. Don't discount the clients who decided *not* to buy your product. Find out why.

Study other successful brands—ones that are well beyond where your business is and ones that are a half-step ahead. When you analyze prominent brands, you can recognize how *you* respond to them from the consumer side, which is helpful intel to leverage. Observe how international brands like Amazon, Disney, The Home Depot, and Netflix are showing up and effectively reaching their target market. What are your favorite brands and why? How does their marketing reach you as the consumer? You will notice strong patterns and can start to apply a similar mindset to your messaging. On the other hand, it's valuable to take a closer look at successful side hustlers who have 12 to 24 months more experience than your side hustle and gauge their results. Here is an exercise that helps you conceptualize how leading business brands develop their niche and effectively reach their target audience.

Ask those same questions about:

▸ Your in-law's woodworking business that has evolved from a side hustle to a front hustle over the last few years
▸ Your buddy who is an electrician in the evenings and weekends and has significantly scaled her revenue over the last 12 months
▸ Your high school friends who have created a strong presence on social media and have grown their part-time home-based businesses
▸ Your neighbor who has been able to go from full time to part time in corporate as they have added more clients to their consulting business

What sticks out to you as general themes in what makes each of these companies (and small business owners) so successful in their reach? Are the differences between each company distinct? Do you have any confusion on what each brand stands for and whether you personally connect or not? Where do you notice more emphasis on personal branding and how effective is it? With these examples in mind, review the responses about your own brand now with more specificity and boldness.

Let's go deeper and do a side-by-side comparison on business branding between Target and Kmart retailers and their growth and relevancy in the twenty-first century. Per Wikipedia they sell parallel product lines in terms of product category.

Target: Beauty and health products, bedding, clothing and accessories, electronics, food, furniture, jewelry, lawn and garden, pet supplies, shoes, small appliances, toys and games

Kmart: Clothing, shoes, linen and bedding, jewelry, accessories, health and beauty products, electronics, toys, food, sporting goods, automotive, hardware, appliances, and pet products

So why is Target booming as the eighth largest retailer in the United States, while Kmart is making a slow, painful descent? At the top of the list, we would put branding. Target is really effective at leveraging the aesthetic intelligence that Pauline Brown speaks to in her book *Aesthetic Intelligence*. They create an experience. In other words, Target creates delight while you are in their store. When you think of Target, you likely think of a modern, clean, energizing experience. It's a place you want to go. Even the typography on their website (heavy use of the classic sans serif font Helvetica, for those who care) delivers a simple, clear element. Target knows its audience and caters to it. When you think of Kmart, you likely think of a place your grandma hangs out to buy dated, cheap, bargain merchandise months in advance for the family Christmas exchange. As helpful as it is to study success stories, it can be as helpful to look at the dinosaurs of an industry to decipher what went wrong.

Think of side hustlers who have done a stellar job of knowing their audience, staying up to date and relevant. Perhaps a real estate agent selling houses that feels current, bringing fresh new perspectives to the social media space versus someone who is struggling to do so with templated direct messages and a formal suit and tie headshot on their business cards and Linkedin bio. If it were a physical picture it would be dusty.

Do research in the market. Put time and effort into studying market trends. You can conduct your own surveys, poll your social media audience, ask your current clientele for their feedback, and leverage existing data and studies that have already been done. However, try not to allow yourself to be bound to those trends. What could you do differently or even better than successful brands in your industry? Airbnb, Facebook, and Uber exist because they asked this question. We discuss differentiation and branding a little later in this chapter.

A practical example for doing detective work if you are getting into the short-term rental game would be to take a close look at why some properties are always booked on VRBO or Airbnb and why some clearly need help. What are the differences in the descriptions, features, photos, reviews? This gives you valuable data versus just your feeling on what works.

Assess if your product or service will legitimately reach the accurate target market.

- ▸ Do your potential clients have the resources to buy your product?
- ▸ Is your product easily accessible to them? Perceived accessibility is hugely important.
- ▸ Will they view your product as a means to help fulfill a need or connect the dots on how your product will benefit them?

You may also build a customer profile and create a brand avatar that is your brand personified. Your avatar represents your target audience and is your ideal end user in character form. This exercise works for any type of business and ensures your ideal audience is tangible and streamlined for yourself, your employees (or future employees), or anyone else you work with behind the scenes. For example, when we had a professional build our website, we had them look at our customer profile and branding guide so there was continuity with the final product. We also had our videographer for content creation, photographer for brand images, and designer for our office space do the same. Give your avatar names—make them come to life so when you think about your business and your brand you are speaking directly to your target market. Our brand avatars are Will and Mallory. They are cool, obviously.

Build Your Story

Brands don't come alive with bullet point lists of adjectives like you see on a poorly written résumé . . . some of the best brands are communicated through stories. Studies have shown that we are motivated toward action through story. Stories let us apply an idea to our own lives. When we can see ourselves in a great story, we are more likely to take some sort of action moving forward, even if it's just choosing between spaghetti sauces at the grocery store. Speaking of spaghetti sauce, Carrie is a huge sucker for Newman's Own. Paul Newman's face on every jar of pasta sauce, the story behind his mission, and knowing that 100 percent of his profits (after tax) go toward his foundation keep her buying. Newman is a great example of making his brand personal. In a different way, take Nike. There isn't one exclusive face that represents the brand, but their marketing team habitually uses success stories as their narrative to inspire athletes and active people in an unparalleled way. One can effectively see themselves in their moving story campaigns. As a result, they focus very little on features or attributes at all because their storytelling sells their products for them. You want their story to be your story, therefore you buy their shoes.

So What Makes an Effective Story?

▶ **Tell an actual story.** An effective story demonstrates an evolution and pulls your audience in, bringing them with you on your journey. Your audience can see themselves in your story, relate to it even in some small way. As a literal example, Airbnb uses the stories, testimonials, and experiences of their customers to become relatable to future customers. Their users, hosts, and guests are the brand, thereby amplifying the overall user experience through the voices of real-life storytellers.

▶ **Incorporate your brand personality with your own personality.** Tell your audience the essence of your brand through how you share the story. Use your voice. As an example, our brand would be described as empowering, challenging, confident, and adventurous. We have woven those themes through how we conduct business and our marketing strategy through the content we create on social media, our website, our logo, and our business values. We hope those we have done business with would affirm these brand attributes, as they reflect who we are as individuals, as well as our business brand.

Once you have pinpointed your brand personality, weave it into your story, imagery, packaging, website, content creation, and overall vibe. Each individual experiences your brand differently, *but* the way you convey it should be congruent.

▶ **Be honest.** Your story should be accurate and representative. It shouldn't be inflated or mirror another brand, as this breaks trust. The Honest Company, which sells nontoxic, eco-friendly baby products, ran into trouble in 2017 with allegations of misleading ingredients in some of their products. The bad publicity definitely took a toll, especially for a company whose name and mission center around honesty and transparency.

We know a "successful" man who runs a high-ticket coaching business. Many consider him an influencer based on his social media presence, and he touts himself as an authority in the small business coaching realm. He brings a lot of flash on the surface, selling his services at a premium. But based on a wide range of client testimonials shared with us in confidence, very few results are driven by the quality of his work. When it comes to how you position yourself in the marketplace, be candid about the tangible results you are genuinely able to provide.

▶ **Use personal anecdotes.** The more your customer can see themselves in your story, the better. The most compelling stories are both personal and visual. Let's say you run a personal injury law firm. When telling your story, you might go into detail about how a former client had to decide between feeding their kids or paying their medical bills. Describe them, name them, and paint a picture of how you helped them through a tragic situation. Your potential clients can identify with that story.

Burt's Bees is a great example of effective storytelling. From their origin story of two hitchhikers hitting it off and making candles together, to a focus on the bees behind their products, Burt's Bees uses compelling visuals and personal details to draw customers into their story. When you hear their story, you involuntarily visualize what it might have looked like for two hitchhikers to make candles together. You can hear the buzz of the bees. Now that you have a visual attached to Burt's Bees (especially if no one else in the skin care category has that visual) that sticks in your mind and can't easily be removed (consciously or unconsciously).

▶ **Share your WHY.** Pulling people in with what made you start your side hustle in the first place is a big part of storytelling. As an example, "I was allergic to all the makeup from the big department stores, so I made my own with essential oils. . . ." Bringing people into your process creates a bridge and serious relatability when you're sharing with the right target audience.

▶ **Be compelling.** Use words that work. Ever noticed how certain words resonate momentarily while others linger and sit with you? The same goes with your brand story. It can either be a quick pass through in someone's brain or stick like duct tape and actually impact. Identify words that evoke feelings while highlighting your brand's idiosyncrasies throughout your story. Make it *pop*. Think of the approach of Dollar Shave Club and why it resonates so much. Its lead commercial asks, "Are our blades any good?" to which the answer goes, "No, our blades are f**king great." This brand has created messaging that its audience relates to: men's frustration and fatigue buying overpriced razors, not just a product.

As Guy Kawasaki and Peg Fitzpatrick share in their book *The Art of Social Media*, "Success favors the bold as well as interesting on social media, so don't hesitate to express your feelings and agenda. People voluntarily followed you; they can voluntarily unfollow you if they don't like what you share." Put in another way, give the right people, your intended audience, a chance at finding you by speaking your truth!

▶ **Be easily understandable.** In Donald Miller's book *Building a Story Brand: Clarify Your Message So Customers Will Listen,* he speaks to our human nature of taking the path of least resistance as consumers. If your audience has to decode your brand and story, know that they probably won't. They will move on without understanding what your company is about and how it could help them. Make your messaging simple and straightforward—don't make your potential customers do extra work. For instance, we know a lot of intelligent, technical entrepreneurs who have great products and services, but the way they convey their brand and message is way over the heads of the average human being. Confusing narratives create a disconnect and equate to missed opportunities for business.

As an example, we know someone who started a pet daycare side business. He has a degree in veterinary science and even does behavioral training with his client's pets when he takes them out for a walk. However, his story and branding would lead you to believe the only thing he does is let your dog outside to water the fire hydrant. There's a real gap and missed opportunity when people don't totally understand what you do, the extent of your expertise, or how your business can benefit them.

> **If your audience has to decode your brand and story, know that they probably won't.**

Once you have developed the story that easily communicates how you and your brand are unique (as long as you actually are), no one can take that away from you! Your story is not static; it can change over time. It's an evolution and you are heavily involved in the process as it's you; it's yours! As you craft your story it is important to know where to share it.

Create a Plan to Reach Your Audience

Now that you have identified where your target market hangs out, and you've got a compelling story to tell, it is imperative that you show up to said space with a strong plan based on your business goals. For many it may be online, for others in person, but for most it will be both. Whether it's your local area, the Northeast region, Instagram, or Facebook, figure out WHERE you want to anchor yourself as you identify HOW to engage, add value, and to represent you and your business.

Develop Your Road Map

Take time to think about the following questions to develop your road map.

- ▶ Which environments will you leverage?
- ▶ What is your purpose in each environment or platform?
- ▶ What is your content strategy, and how does it reflect your expertise and the problems that you solve better than others?
- ▶ If online, how often and when will you be posting content?
- ▶ What type of engagement are you working to create? What does a win look like?
- ▶ What is your overall theme and vibe (see previous section)?
- ▶ What is your brand's personality? Are you effectively conveying your story? If your brand was a person, would you like them or want to be friends?
- ▶ What is your end goal?

Once you have identified the answers to these questions, you want to dig into setting up your profiles, assuming you are tapping into social media. To get started you primarily need an account with a solid bio that represents you well.

Creating a Compelling Social Media Profile

1. **Have a solid profile photo.** It should look like the current you, not the 2016 version of you. Your photo should emit "I'm someone you want to get to know better" energy. Streamline your photo, handle and name on your social media accounts so people can find you on other platforms more easily.

2. **Many platforms give you space for a headline.** The amount of characters you can use varies, so be smart with this real estate. Your tagline should pop, as this and your photo are where people make snap judgments on whether they want to look at your page further. Reel them in!

3. **Create an authentic and representative bio summary.** Referencing the previous branding questions goes a long way for crafting this section.

4. **Flex your muscles.** This is a great space to share the highlights of your story. Pull people in so they can see themselves in your narrative or see you as a solution for their challenges.

5. **Work to get reviews and recommendations on your page.** This approach builds so much credibility for your brand, and when happy customers do the bragging for you, it carries a different weight.

6. **Build out your profile.** Certain platforms enable you to pin key posts, photos, articles, or videos as your highlights, so put thought into what you want the primary focal point to be on your page. Work to keep all of this "on brand" so your message is clear and fluid. This is free advertising space—work it.

7. **Be sure to have a second pair of eyes give you feedback on your profile.** We all make mistakes and have oversights.

The Power of Content Creation

As mentioned, social media can be a huge asset for your personal branding and business. But you don't just make an account and instantly attract the masses. Effective social media strategies take work—smart work. We highly recommend leveraging content creation paired with strong branding, which can entail a wide range of video content, storytelling, text posts, photographic imagery, blogging, articles, and live broadcasts. These are all forms of content marketing that push out value through content distribution in an effort to generate attention, leads, and revenue over time.

But why content, specifically? Content creation is a fantastic way to expose yourself in the best way possible, as well as your brand, to a virtual audience (for low cost). Effective content creation makes people feel like they've gotten something for free . . . something that adds value to them. You are giving your audience a sneak peek or trailer of what working with you would look like and the benefits they can gain from your expertise! And we are in an age where people want to know the face behind the brand. Your content itself is a powerful branding mechanism and can also build you a following because your audience comes back for more value, more free advice, and more ideas. And if they don't need your paid services or product now, they know to come to you when they do!

Content creation is also an opportunity to engage your growing community in a meaningful way. Messaging for the sake of messaging can do more damage than good. As you engage on social media, it is essential to have anchoring principles for why you are there, what your goals are, how much time you want to spend there, and exactly what you want to be spending your time doing, as this can be very helpful in giving you both limits and a roadmap. Here are some ideas to help you understand the role content plays in your branding and how to develop it for your target market.

Amplify Your Differentiator

Dig deep to better convey your unique slight edge by writing down and answering these questions:

- What does your brand do best?
- Why do you do what you do best?
- How are you different from the rest of humanity?

- ▸ What is your unique angle?
- ▸ What are your leading principles and values?
- ▸ What brand strengths of yours are extraordinary?
- ▸ What is your brand's deeper vision? How can others rally behind this vision and be part of your mission?

For example, TOMS Shoes does a standout job of answering these questions loud and clear through their branding and clarity of vision. Carrie here. I know that every time I buy their shoes, which is often, that one-third of their annual net profit goes toward designated causes. I also know they value sustainability and equality of opportunity. They tie their products to causes and make their consumers feel part of something bigger than footwear. And this keeps me coming back!

If you're struggling to decipher how you are different, then that should be a red flag to you to take a hot minute and a step back. It might be time to pull in a branding professional to help you decode why a consumer should take action and join your movement. If you are unsure, then why would anyone else be sure? Confidence and clarity are key.

Organize Your Ideas Through Ideation

What is the objective? What topics do you have expert authority around? What are your values? What are the specs on your audience and target market? Come up with a brainstorming list of core topics and subtopics you can speak to. Be sure that 100 percent of your content isn't specific to your industry. Add human elements and humor to the mix and shake things up! For the love, share a random, funny story sometime and see what happens.

Generate Content through Bulk Creation

When you are in your creative flow, don't slow down. For maximum efficiency, create multiple pieces of content at a time. Feel free to change outfits or backdrops for variation. This helps put you in a position of strength, as you'll have a lot of content to pull from as you post.

Outsource

As discussed in earlier chapters, figure out what makes sense to have someone else handle. For example, you probably can't outsource speaking on a podcast; however, there are areas such as adding subtitles to your content or pushing it out on different platforms that could easily be done by someone else. Referrals go a long way, so poll your community and find effective people within your price point. Don't forget there is often room for negotiation or swapping services.

Value

Add a ton of it. Think abundance and give away loads of free content. This might feel counterintuitive, but the more people benefit from your content and know your mad skills, the more likely they will seek you out for more as well as promote the heck out of you! Don't get in your own way of creating viral traffic by holding your cards too close to your chest.

Have a Call to Action

Be sure your content is actionable, meaning someone has something they can do with the information you shared with them. Ask yourself, *How can my audience implement this idea, strategy or thought?* If you're not sure, you want to go back to the drawing board.

Develop a Cadence with Your Posts

The more you keep showing up, the more others will too. If you plan and execute on throwing the party, the guest list might be light initially, but it will continue to build (assuming you plug away with our other suggestions). Frequency matters!

Execute

Once you post, be sure to invest time into the backend work of fanning the flame on your traction through responding to comments.

In addition to creating and posting your original content, we recommend four things you can do to maximize your impact and create content that connects your brand to your intended audience.

1. **Add connection requests.** You need an audience. Continue building it. Personalized invitations can go a long way for getting your requests accepted.
2. **Direct message your new and old connections.** A large piece of building a community is extending a hand or dialogue to those within your network. A friendly hello or candid introduction can go a long way for learning more about your audience as well as

getting people excited about learning more about you (keep in mind this is not an opportunity to mass pitch your network).

3. **Create a prioritized to-do list and use a timer to stay on task if necessary.** The struggle is real. Social media is one of the most distracting places in the world that we go to and attempt to be productive. Your cell phone can be a liability or an asset depending on how you're using it. There is so much opportunity cost in anything you do, so be deliberate, efficient, and efficacious.

> When on social media, deploy the concept of surgical strikes, meaning get in and *get out*. Do what you need to do, and don't get tripped up with all the other inputs and distractions that can become a time suck.

4. **Comment on others' content.** One of the best ways to create visibility and traffic to your own profile is to create impactful noise on other profiles, especially when it's a creator you respect and align with. Be generous and sincere, and add value, and it will draw a ton of positive visibility your way over time. Reposting or sharing other people's content is a great way to show solidarity and build community, assuming you give them credit. There is so much power in reciprocity!

You can have meaningful and different content, but if it isn't positioned the right way, nobody will read it, or worse, the message will be lost in translation. So from a technical standpoint, here are some small but critical things to consider when polishing your content for cyber launch.

▶ **Hook:** Lead with a strong opening line that draws people in! Don't be boring. Your goal is to get people to slow their scroll with your originality and creativity. Observe content that pulls you in and gains your attention and duplicate what fits your style and personality.

▶ **Hashtags:** They help people find you and can become a sticky element of your brand. Include a personal hashtag in your posts so people can start to follow that hashtag specifically. It ultimately creates a library of your content. Also include three to four additional hashtags that are relevant to the topic you are speaking to. Learn how to use them effectively, and they will be a lever for your visibility and reach.

▸ **Tag:** Tag people in your posts, not as a technique but assuming there is relevancy to that person and what you are posting about. Don't be that person who goes ballistic with the tagging strategy. It's not a good look, and isn't typically well received by the people getting overtapped.

▸ **Timing:** Put thought into when people tend to check their feeds. Commute times and lunch times are examples of when people frequently check social. When you factor in different time zones, there are always people on social, so don't overthink it but consider it!

▸ **Variation of posts:** Whether it's video, long form content, articles, images, text post only, listicles, polls, and so on, switch it up and have some variation in your content. It shows range and engages different people differently.

▸ **Include subtitles with video content:** Subtitles create better accessibility, and generally people are way more likely to go through your content if you include them in your video posts. Yes, it takes extra time but it's worth it.

▸ **Create more engagement on your own content:** Get deep in the comments section with your community. When people engage and are ready to talk to you, praise you, or question you—show up! Do your best to be in the thick of the dialogue with prompt turnaround time. Likes and commenting perpetuate the visibility of what you put out.

Ultimately, the goal is to be productive *and* happy, so learn how to leverage your time on social media and simultaneously protect your time—it is a skill and boundaries go a long way. As mentioned, the more you grow and the more visibility your brand creates, you will have an influx of people commenting and direct-messaging you (oftentimes on topics unrelated to your business)! This type of traction is a great sign of growth online; however, you can easily get swept away in the noise. Avoid being at the whim of all the notifications and inbound messages.

▶ **Message people who engage on your posts.** Build bridges with people who are engaging with you. Get to know them better. Keep leaning into relationships.

▶ **Apply analytics—*always*.** For example, if you currently have two followers on Instagram, you may want to go heavier on adding connections initially before diving headfirst into posting content. Follow guidelines and approaches that make practical sense for where you are at on your journey. While online platforms can be really incredible in helping you grow your brand, it's important to also keep in mind it's not one size fits all on social media.

Create Revenue

The goal of any business is to create revenue and ultimately, profit. Whether you are a side-hustling local gardener or a graphic designer by night, your objective is to generate sales (and net profit as talked about in Chapter 7). We have seen many businesses flounder in the process of creating sales, which puts them out of business quickly. For enhancing revenue, we recommend using the following approaches:

1. Be extremely clear on your offering.
2. Make it obvious where people can find you, and make it easy for people to purchase your product or service. This seems apparent, but a lot of new business owners overlook extra hoops they create for their potential customers. How easy is it to access and navigate your website? Add items to the cart? Check out? Remember, your consumer base does *not* want to do extra work to get your product especially when they are not loyal yet.
3. Leverage the heck out of user-generated content. Let people talk. This is clutch! Share positive reviews on your website or on your social media stories. So many consumers are review driven. Give the people what they want! Repost your customers social media posts praising your company. This creates an entirely different dynamic when others are promoting you versus you promoting how awesome you are.

4. Build email lists with monthly newsletters. As mentioned, this is a great way to stay on your customers' radar. Make sure you are actually adding value to them versus creating spam, as you can simultaneously keep them up to date on new and fresh offerings.

5. Develop a strong SEO. Work to grow your visibility and frequency so that you are higher up on search engine pages and so that keywords that are being searched are more frequently and effectively drawing consumers to your page.

6. Use content marketing. Create content so you can answer people's questions and problems for free. This builds confidence as it shows competency, which drives more users to your website and offerings.

7. Leverage paid advertising. There are lots of opportunities for paid advertisements and each have pros and cons. Whether it's paid advertisements on Facebook or Instagram, which can be fairly economical and measurable, or something larger scale, this method can help drive traffic to target individuals who your product or service can specifically help serve.

8. Network like your business depends on it—because it probably does. We have all heard the adage "It's not what you know but who you know." *So who do you know? And who knows you? How can you build on your social capital?* Social media creates a massive opportunity. We know, "Friendships and partnerships on the internet?" We were skeptical too, but that is one of the best places to put your pole in the water and create relationships as well as revenue. But don't exclusively hang out behind your computer, also network live and in the real and show up consistently. Even if someone doesn't currently need your product or service, if you've built familiarity and trust, they will think of you first when they do need your help (or someone in their network does).

9. Be a big advocate and referral source for other people's businesses. The more you give, the more you gain, period. As Daymond John on *Shark Tank* shares, "We're talking tapping into other people's marketing, mind power, and momentum, even other people's manpower. Cross-promote with others' in the industry you operate in. It goes both ways. You promote them. They promote you. It's mutually beneficial and it doesn't cost a thing."

10. Create exceptional customer service and support. This is one of the best ways to separate yourself from the masses. As an example, Carrie here, I recently purchased some clothing online from my friend Tori's boutique. I happened to be heading out of town the next day, and Tori, who is local to me, hand delivered my items to my door so I could be sure to have my new threads for my trip. This is an example of creating a slight edge with your customer base. Small, thoughtful steps create an immense amount of positive, public praise as well as repeat revenue, and is particularly powerful for a small business owner.

11. Collaborate with those in and outside your industry. Podcasting is a great example of this. Both hosting and being a guest can magnify your voice and create a cascade of other opportunities and direct and indirect sales. You are boosting your volume exponentially by broadcasting your value on more microphones and channels. Have a clear call to action and an easy way people can reach out and connect with you and access your offering.

12. Develop an affiliate program! You can incentivize existing customers to refer business your way for cash referrals or credit on their purchases with you. By minimizing their costs or kicking them a commission, they will be more likely to promote you on social media and do word of mouth marketing for you. **We could write a book on this topic and seriously urge you to create an affiliate program. In doing so, others are more likely to add you to their affiliate programs, further diversifying your income options also!**

— — —

No matter which environments you choose to leverage—in person, online, or both (recommended)—know that personal and business branding as well as marketing are areas for *considerable* thought and investment so you represent yourself and your business well, differentiate yourself from others, and broadcast yourself clearly enough so the right people can find you and actually purchase your product or services. Embrace the learning curve and be BOLD. Entrepreneurship does not reward the meek!

CONCLUSION

*The price of anything is the amount
of life you exchange for it.*
—Henry David Thoreau

*I'm convinced that about half of what separates successful
entrepreneurs from the non-successful ones is pure perseverance.*
—Steve Jobs

We hope this book has propelled you forward in developing a stronger mindset and clarity around a vision for your future—supporting you in building the *life you want, as you define it.* By challenging yourself to clarify what your Life Vision is, you can reverse engineer and chart a real course to arrive at said destination. A side hustle provided us the bridge necessary to make our own journey successful and fulfilling—we believe it can for you as well.

As you continue pursuing your side hustle, keep in mind the following thoughts:

1. **Commit or recommit to making your side hustle a priority.**
   There are scores of reasons to elevate building a side hustle, and almost infinite distractions to keep you from prioritizing it.

Commit yourself to making your move with definitiveness and a sense of adventure; *it will be worth what you must exchange for it.*

2. **Revisit, sharpen, and crystalize your Life Vision.** How do you truly want to live? What do you value? Where do you want to be 10 years from now? How does your side hustle fit into this vision? This is the driver for your work, dedication, and resiliency.

3. **Determine WHO *already* lives this way.** Who has already made it to your destination? Who else is on a similar journey? Make these people a part of your life. *Fight* to get into the inner circle of the people you respect and want to emulate. Fight even harder to gain their expertise and respect. Observe them. Watch for patterns. Ask questions. Be curious and humble as you lean on and learn from them.

4. **Choose or enhance your WHAT.** Evaluate your side hustling options, keeping the WHO at the forefront, and consider what most realistically facilitates manifesting your Life Vision. Will you innovate or use established systems? How critical is passive or progressive-passive income? Do you need your business or product to be your passion? Keep in mind your first side hustle doesn't have to be your last.

5. **Get your LIFESET in order!** As best as possible, put yourself in an optimal setup for long term *sustainability* by making solid career and financial decisions. And don't forget about your health, relationships, spiritual walk and recreation! Remember, it doesn't have to be in "perfect" order, as it never will be.

6. **Hierarchize self-development.** Begin intentionally owning and raising your self-image. Use experiential learning as a tool to develop the necessary skills to communicate effectively, as well as influence others. You will struggle to scale anything beyond where your personal belief caps you. *Use feedback, mistakes, and experiences as tools to learn rather than symbols of your failure.* Fail, learn, adjust, take more action, fail, learn, adjust, and take more action, again. Repeat for 5 to 40 years, as necessary. Rage against ever becoming bitter or jaded on the journey.

7. **Be aware of the typical side hustle pain points.** You'll encounter plenty of challenges. Be eyes wide open for spotting common hurdles so you can handle them with more grace and grit. Recall, this is an *adventure*, not a stroll in the park.

8. **Execute like a CEO.** Arm and equip yourself with the proper mindset for making significantly more and higher-caliber decisions as a business owner. Learn how to isolate and develop this as a skill—it is paramount and one in which most have had little, if any, formal training. Give yourself the gift of decisiveness.

9. **Choose your inner circle wisely.** Poor decisions when choosing business partners, employees, or other key relationships can cost you heavily, in both money and time. Evaluate which type of support you need and surround yourself with those of high skill, character, and values that align with your own. Use an individual's historical performance as a measure of these attributes, not their personality.

10. **Funding your venture.** Having enough capital is crucial. Without it, much of our other advice and your efforts are rendered useless. Consider all your options, develop a plan, and consult experts prior to moving forward when making major financial decisions.

11. **Marketing and branding.** Without sufficient sales and top-line revenue you are dead in the water. Make this a priority and learn to effectively use marketing and branding to amplify and leverage your efforts. Realize most people only think of a few adjectives when it comes to *you* and *your brand*. Do not be *forgettable*! Differentiate yourself by overdelivering value and leading with relationships.

If we haven't emphasized this enough, entrepreneurship is hard. *Really freaking challenging*—for most of us anyway. As a matter of fact, just getting this book written and published was a wild experience in and of itself. But for us the more paramount question is not, "Is it difficult?" but, "Is the challenge worth the reward?" Our answer: *Hell to the Yes*.

You will eventually have to face many things you don't want to face. You will have to be more honest with yourself than you ever have—and in ways you never have. Entrepreneurship tears you open mentally and emotionally and forces out what you're made of—whether you like it or not.

A major challenge for many neophyte business owners is they expect to *love every aspect* of entrepreneurship. Many feel they are doing something wrong when their honeymoon phase ends, and every minute isn't lovable. It is simply *not* so. Like the rewards of a good marriage (or any interdependent relationship), you have to push *through* what makes it frustrating or challenging. This is where learning truly starts . . . in the be-coming through the process. You will have to fight past the mundane aspects of building a company. The unglamorous stuff. The redundant stuff. The stuff such as filing your taxes or completing your unemployment insurance forms. You know, *the stuff that puts people on stages and book covers.*

There will be days when you have to resist quitting. There will be times when you wish you didn't have that extra spark, bigger dream, or vision, or that you hadn't taken the red pill. That you could just crawl back into the Matrix and make it all go away.

Keep. The. Hammer. Down.

Oftentimes, we can enroll others to rally around our cause and mission not just because of our technical genius-ness, but because of our spirit and attitude in the face of challenges, the clarity of our purpose, and how we move and navigate with an elevated sense of faith and belief. It is frequently our command over our own emotions, thinking, and actions that can inspire our partners, employees, co-owners, or investors more than a specific business strategy. There's a reason people adore fairytales, fantasies, and Hollywood stories of the underdog coming out on top (please go watch *Cinderella Man*—after you finish this chapter). Humanity *craves* it. We have multibillion-dollar movies and billion-dollar industries full of stories just to relish in observing *someone else's* victory.

> **For as long as human history has endured there have been those *who love* great stories, and those who *make* great stories.**

Every grand story is made so by the level of challenge someone had to not only endure, but also conquer—and the greater the challenge, the greater the story.

So the question is, *What will your story be?* What example will you not just *tell* your children about, but *be* for them? And if not your own children, then for your friends, your community, or yourself? There is only one person who can answer that question.

Perhaps it's time you start answering.

We wish you exactly as much in rewards as you are willing to embrace in challenge and *ad*venture. No more and no less, because it will be exactly what you have *earned*—exactly what you have *purchased*.

One of the main reasons we wrote this book is because we felt deeply and earnestly we had something to say that could be of genuine service. We hope we have been, and we hope you are willing to return serve.

Stay focused on WHAT and WHO matter most.

And *enjoy the grind*.

C&C

RECOMMENDED READING

These are books that have helped us in the various stages of our side hustle journey. We've referenced many of these authors throughout the book, but we thought it would be helpful to list them here for your convenience.

Happy reading,

C&C

The Seven Habits of Highly Effective People by Stephen R. Covey

Crucial Conversations: Tools for Talking When Stakes Are High by Alan Switzler, Joseph Grenny and Ron McMillan

The Go Giver by Bob Burg and John David Mann

100 Side Hustles by Chris Guillebeau

Cash Flow Quadrant by Robert Kiyosaki

Atomic Habits by James Clear

The Compound Effect by Darren Hardy

Principles by Ray Dalio

Eat That Frog by Brian Tracy

The 4-Hour Work Week by Timothy Ferris

First Things First by Stephen R Covey

The Millionaire Next Door by Thomas J. Stanley

The Total Money Makeover by Dave Ramsey

Happy Money by Ken Honda

Think and Grow Rich by Napoleon Hill

Mindset: The New Psychology of Success by Carol Dweck

21 Irrefutable Laws of Leadership by John C. Maxwell

The Four Agreements: A Practical Guide to Personal Freedom by Don
Miguel Ruiz

No Matter What by Sam Silverstein

The E-Myth Revisited by Michael E. Gerber

Brand Intervention by David Brier

The Art of Social Media by Guy Kawasaki and Peg Fitzpatrick

Building a Story Brand by Donald Miller

Building Distinctive Assets by Jenni Romaniuk

Brand Seduction by Daryl Weber

Aesthetic Intelligence by Pauline Brown

How Brands Grow by Byron Sharpe

How to Win Friends and Influence People by Dale Carnegie

INDEX

ABOUT THE AUTHORS

Craig Clickner is a former commercial banker and **Carrie Bohlig** is a former preschool teacher. Together they used the power of side hustles to step away from their traditional jobs and create both the financial security, and autonomy over their time they envisioned. They have several businesses including Tandem Consulting; Click Global LLC; CC Global LLC; LWCB Holdings LLC; non-profit, Tandem Giving, Inc; and their podcast, *Tandem Talks*. They speak to thousands of aspiring entrepreneurs and independent contractors annually about the importance of self-empowerment and business ownership—and how to use entrepreneurship to not just make extra income but to elevate the quality of your life.

Craig & Carrie reside in the Madison, WI area with their two young children and Swimmy, the family fish.

A portion of the author's royalties from this book will be donated to their charity, Tandem Giving, Inc.